Steamboats on the Chena

The Founding and Development of Fairbanks, Alaska

Steamboats on the Chena

The Founding and Development of Fairbanks, Alaska

Basil C. Hedrick
and
Susan C. Savage

Epicenter Press Inc.
Fairbanks, Alaska

FOR “CAP” HEDRICK

Cover Design by Marc Roberson

Library of Congress Catalog Card Number 87-83742

Epicenter Press Inc.
P.O. Box 60529, Fairbanks, AK 99706
Printed in the United States of America

Contents

Preface

Fairbanks was founded on the banks of the water, grew on the banks of the water, and thrived or foundered in its early years in direct relationship to the fortunes of the steamboats which plied the Chena Slough. There can be no doubt: Fairbanks was — and is — a river town. Its steamboats were as real, as important and as romantic as any of those that plied the rivers of the "Lower 48."

The first steamboat came up the Tanana River to the Chena Slough and hence upstream to a point purportedly 100 miles above the site of the future Fairbanks. This occurred in 1898; the boat was the *Tanana Chief.* She passed the *Lavelle Young*, trying urgently to find a way over a sand bar into the Tanana River that same year. It was the *Lavelle Young* that would in 1901 carry E.T. Barnette to the place where he would found Fairbanks.

Steamboating evokes wildly romantic images, particularly in the minds of those who have never worked on one. Never mind the noise, the dirt, the heat, the cold, the wet discomfort, the long hours, the cramped quarters and the mosquitoes. Yet, who does not thrill to the sight of a majestic wood palace coming around the bend of the river, wheel turning, smoke billowing, steam "chuffing." It is a strange world of love and hate for a steamboat person. At the end of a long navigation season, a steamboat crew member will swear that he will never set foot on one of the Godforsaken scows again — at least until next spring.

The smoke-and-spark-spewing leviathans weaved the cloth of exploration, founding, and development in much of what is today the State of Alaska. In this publication, the authors trace their role in the founding and development of the City of Fairbanks. For those who will wonder: We refrain from saying "sternwheeler" as a generic word for steamboat since various sidewheelers were used on many Interior rivers, including both the Upper Tanana and the Chena.

What if Barnette's original boat, the *Arctic Boy*, had not sunk? What if the founder of Fairbanks had, indeed, come up the Yukon and Tanana in a shallow-draft boat instead of the *Lavelle Young*? Would he have chugged right on by the mouth of the Chena Slough and up the Tanana to Tanana Crossing (Tanacross) — where he intended to go? Even if a smaller vessel had come up the Chena and gone up to where it rejoined with the Tanana, thus by-passing Bates Rapids, would Fairbanks even have been founded? Moot questions, but interesting speculation. Low water, boat wrecks, too-big boats, and pilots unfamiliar with the Upper Tanana: these all played a part in the founding of Fairbanks. There is one story attributed to Barnette which has often been thought to be just that — a story — but which turns out to be true. He had tried to persuade Captain Adams, co-owner and captain of the *Lavelle Young*, that by going up the Chena, one eventually could get back to the Tanana River, by-passing the rapids and arriving safely much further up-stream. Barnette claimed to have been told this by one or more Indians (depending on which version you like) and, sure enough, it was true at that time. If the water had been just a little higher or if Adams had persevered just a bit more in seeking a channel through the Chena, the deed could have been accomplished.

This research has been interesting, entertaining, at times amusing, often frustrating, and — seen retrospectively — fun. We sincerely hope that the reader will enjoy the work as much as we have enjoyed putting it together.

Acknowledgments

As with any written work, there are many individuals responsible for the end product. Therefore, while acknowledging mistakes of fact as ours, we want to thank Niilo Koponen, Dermot Cole, Linda Buechler, Renee Blahuta, Paolo Greer, Dale Stirling and Bruce Haldeman for their contributions to the labors.

Further gratitude goes to Mary Beth Smetzer for her most important help, especially in the research aspects of the study; to Barry McWayne for his outstanding help in photography; to Frank and Dolly Young for their reminiscences; to Art Knutson for his insights to Alaska river travel and for access to his notes; to Jim Swift of the *Waterways Journal* for making available the *Journal's* library, morgue, and files — not to mention his wonderful memory of things past; to John Neal Hoover of the St. Louis Mercantile Library Association, who accommodated us by retrieving books and papers from all over the library — the collection being under reorganization — thus saving the day for us in a very real way; to Candy Waugaman for her cheerful sharing of her outstanding collection of Alaskana; and to the Fairbanks North Star Borough Library staff and administration for their many kindnesses.

To Sheila Carlson for her immense fortitude in preparing various versions of the manuscript and for her cheery approach to the subject; and to Hazel Daro for her organizational talents in keeping things rolling, we are indebted. We are grateful to Dixon Sims for his cartographic skills. To Bill Hanable and Jo Antonson for sharing freely of their considerable knowledge of Alaska history — thank you. Dave Norton was a constant source of moral support and provided much enthusiasm.

Susan Pickel-Hedrick and Jerry Savage are appreciated for their advice, their critical readings of the manuscript at various stages and for their patience.

Original research for this publication was supported by a grant from the State of Alaska, Alaska Historical Commission. The authors are, of course, responsible for all statements herein, whether of fact or opinion. (1120/FY 86-Role of the Steamboat in the Founding and Development of Fairbanks, Alaska.)

Introduction

Prior to 1741, what is today Alaska was essentially *terra incognita* to all but the Native peoples residing there: the Aleuts, Eskimos, Tlingits, Haidas, and Athabascans. Alaska is immense; it was not until the incursion of the various missionaries in the 18th century that the Native peoples of the Bering Sea acquired any real knowledge about the peoples of Southeast Alaska.

Alaska's recorded history began in 1741, when Vitus Bering, a Danish navigator in the service of Russia, sailed east from Siberia and landed in Alaska. This was Bering's second voyage to the New World. He previously had proven that the two continents were separated by discovering the strait today bearing his name, but he was unable to land on that voyage owing to fog. In mid-July of 1741, he landed on the southern coast near the mouth of the Copper River. Bering died as a result of shipwreck on the return voyage to Russia. However, some of the sea otter pelts which were returned to the Old Country fetched the highest prices of any fur of the day and, soon, the Russians were regularly sailing to explore Alaska waters and to capture otters, fur seals and blue foxes, all of which were abundant. This fur trade formed the basis of the Russian-American economy.

The first permanent settlement in Alaska was founded by Grigori Shelekhov at Three Saints Bay on the island of Kodiak in 1784. However, as early as 1779, the Russians were looking at Sitka, far to the south in the Alexander Archipelago, as a possible center of operations and, in 1804, Sitka (then New Archangel) was permanently founded after the local Indians were defeated by Aleksandr Andreyevich Baranov. It prospered and soon became the most important town in Russian America and a port for foreign vessels in the northwest coast and China trade. After Baranov's retirement in 1818, the Russian American Company continued to rule the area until the end of 1861.

Other European powers, having learned of Russia's activities in northern America, began to stir. Spain, Britain and France all asserted certain claims at different times. Still, wars back at home, incredibly long supply-lines, lack of forces and ships and a general feeling that Alaska was not worth the effort eventually led these nations to abandon their claims. By 1866, Russia was willing to listen to William H. Seward, the U.S. secretary of state, when he agitated for purchase of Alaska. By terms of the treaty signed on March 30, 1867, the sum of $7,200,000 (less than two cents per acre) was paid to Russia for its possessions in America, and on October 18, 1867, the formal transfer took place at Sitka.

Juneau was designated the capital city in 1900, but effective government remained in Sitka until 1906. The U.S. Congress authorized a limited territorial government for Alaska in 1912 and the first Territorial Legislature convened at Juneau on March 3, 1913.

Gold was discovered as early as 1880 in the Gastineau Channel area, just off Juneau, and the first influx of settlers since the purchase built the towns of Juneau, Douglas, and Treadwell near the mines. Thus, the foundation was laid for one of Alaska's major industries — gold mining. Prospectors fanned out from the Juneau area and went into the Interior to prospect the Upper Yukon country. The rich gold mines around Fortymile were discovered in 1886. The Birch Creek deposits found in 1882 fostered the town of Circle City. The fabulous gold lode of the Klondike, in Canada's Yukon Territory, was struck in 1896. Nome followed in 1899 and, as we will see, Felix Pedro's discovery of gold in the Fairbanks area led to the founding of the town in 1902.

The earliest exploration of the Interior of Alaska by white men probably took place along the Yukon River and resulted in the establishment of fur-trading posts by the Russian-American Company, the Hudson's Bay Company, the Western Fur and Trading Company, and various others. [1] It was from these bases that the early exploration of the Tanana River, primarily by canoe and other small boats, took place (see Map 1). Arthur Harper, a manager of an Alaska Commercial Company Trading Post, and a Mr.

Bates, an Englishman, were the first white people known to have descended the Tanana River. Sometime between 1874 and 1878 these two men crossed over from the Yukon River near Eagle to the Tanana River approximately 50 miles downstream from present-day Tanacross. From there they quickly descended the Tanana in a crude skin boat in 10 days to where that stream joins the Yukon. [2] In 1878, Harper and another employee of the Alaska Commercial Company, Alfred Mayo, went up the Tanana River perhaps 250 to 300 miles. This put them near where the present-day Chena River joins the Tanana. It was on this trip that they may have set up a trading post on the Tanana River about 48 miles above its mouth. [3]

In 1885, Lieutenant Henry T. Allen with two enlisted men and two prospectors reached the Tanana River by going up the Copper River and through the Suslota Pass. Being low on supplies, they descended the river in nine days, but as they traveled, Lieutenant Allen made sketches and the first reliable maps of the Tanana Valley. From his notes, Allen and his party appear to have camped near the mouth of the Chena River, but they did not see it.[4]

In the 1890s prospecting was developing along the Yukon River. There was some interest in the Tanana River, a dangerous river for small craft to navigate owing to rapids, hidden snags and rocks, "sweepers," and log jams. Thus, few tried to boat upstream from the Yukon River. Reaching the Tanana from the south or the north was difficult because of mountainous terrain and boggy ground. Another deterrent was rumors that the Tanana Indians were not friendly.

Driven by the urge for gold, prospectors explored the Tanana Valley anyway. By the late 1890s, prospecting parties were traveling overland from the Yukon on the few Indian trails, or on trails that were developed by the prospectors. Some of the individuals even then were prospecting on the Upper Chena. Still hampered by the lack of a supply source, they had to pack in their food and supplies on their backs. When they ran short of supplies, they headed back to Circle City, a distance, depending on their location, of 125 to 300 miles. There, they replenished their stocks and then returned over the trails to their prospecting in the Tanana Valley.

As the population grew along the Yukon, especially after the successful gold strike in the Klondike, the U.S. government became concerned about the easier access to the Interior of Alaska. A route was needed to maintain law and order, to obtain easier communication (telegraph and mail), and to cross only American territory. The military set out several expeditions to explore routes into the Interior.

In 1898, Alfred H. Brooks participated in a surveying expedition down the Tanana. While descending the river, they saw prospectors along the way and saw cord wood, presumably for a steamboat, stacked at the Wood River. On August 29, Brooks reported seeing the *Tanana Chief* and an unnamed steamboat going up the river. [5]

Later that summer, as a part of a major expedition of exploration, Lieutenant J.C. Castner, along with two or three men, traveled up from the Susitna region, via the Matanuska River. These men eventually came to the Tanana River, crossed it, and tried to ascend the Goodpaster River. Running short of supplies, they had to turn around and go back down the Goodpaster to the Tanana. There, they came across a camp where the Indians took them in. The Natives fed and clothed them and eventually escorted them downriver. When they got to the mouth of the Chena River in early October, they found an old chief at his fish camp. While his men stayed at the fish camp with the chief, Lieutenant Castner and the other Indians went up the Chena because the Indians had heard there were two steamboats upstream. It is estimated that where the present-day Little Chena River merges with the Chena River, they encountered two small steamboats, the *Tanana Chief* (a 20-ton boat) and the *Potlatch*. Aboard were some 18 prospectors, with their supplies, conducting an extended search of the Upper Chena, the Chatanika Valley and surrounding area. [6] The newcomers stayed that winter and through the next summer prospecting,[7] but they were unsuccessful since they were not looking for deep-buried (lode) gold. Their steamboats appear to be the first to have navigated the Chena River.

PART I: Founding and Early Development of Fairbanks (1901-1905)

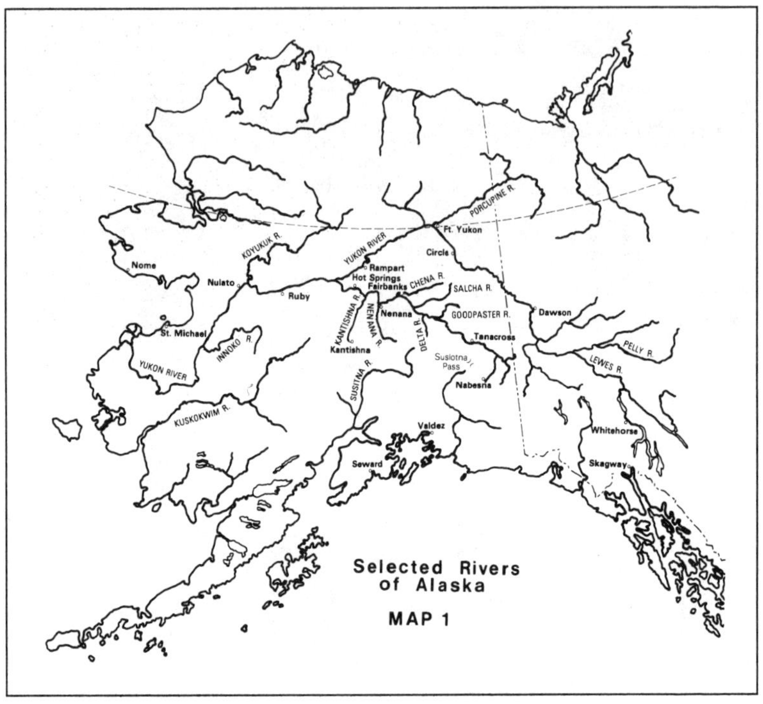

AFTER ALASKA'S PURCHASE from Russia in 1867, many of Alaska's 3,000 rivers were used as "highways" for travel and exploration from the coast into the vast Interior regions.

For more than half a century, steamboats were the main form of transportation until the coming of the railroads, construction of the first crude overland roads and, finally, the arrival of the airplane — all contributing to the demise of the colorful steamboat era in Alaska.

This is the story of a river town, Fairbanks, founded, fed and fostered by steamboats its first two decades after the turn of the century.

C. Waugaman Collection.

The *Lavelle Young*, the *Isabelle* and the *Rock Island* land at Fairbanks, circa 1904. The *Rock Island* was built near Seattle by a father-son team from the Kahlke Boat Yard of Rock Island, Ill. Co-author Basil Hedrick's father, a long-time riverman, later became a friend of the younger Kahlke after he returned to Illinois.

F. L. Hess 55, U.S. Geological Survey

Various steamboats including the *Jenny M* (with a home port of Philadelphia!), the *Isabelle*, the *Koyukuk*, the *Tanana* and the *Florence S* are tied up at Fairbanks on July 29, 1904, in this view from the north bank of the Chena Slough.

Bunnell Collection, University of Alaska Fairbanks archives

The *Lavelle Young* is most prominent among the steamboats tied up at the Fairbanks waterfront in this photograph taken in about 1905. This steamer brought E.T. Barnette, founder of Fairbanks, to the townsite in 1901 under the command of Capt. C.W. Adams. The *Lavelle Young* originally was used as a dredgeboat on the Koyukuk and Kuskowkim rivers.

Bunnell Collection, UAF archives

The waterfront at Fairbanks, as seen in about 1905. Note the N.C. Company building, still standing today.

Bunnell Collection, UAF archives

This was the view from the north bank of the Chena Slough in about 1905, overlooking one of the many bridges that crossed the slough in the early days of Fairbanks.

Bunnell Collection, UAF archives

Several steamboats tied up at the Fairbanks waterfront helped battle the fire which destroyed much of the city on May 22, 1906.

Bunnell Collection, UAF archives

Despite the best efforts of many of the city's residents, the heart of Fairbanks was gutted in the great fire of May 1906. Rebuilding started almost immediately.

Bunnell Collection, UAF archives

Nothing but smoking debris remained in downtown Fairbanks after the fire of May 22, 1906.

Selid-Bassoc Collection, UAF archives

The steamer *Lotta Talbot*, a refrigerator boat selling fresh meat, was a regular visitor to Fairbanks. Eventually bought by the Weichler Brothers of Fairbanks, the sternwheeler was sunk during the 1906 breakup at Fairbanks, then burned to the waterline later that year in a fire that also destroyed the Riverside Hotel.

C.E. Ellsworth 33, U.S. Geological Survey

The Dominion Commercial Co. warehouse is seen on the right in May 1910. Steamboats on the dock include the *Tanana* and the *Evelyn.*

Erskine Collection, UAF archives

These Northern Navigation Co. boats wintered at Fairbanks in 1907: the *Tanana*, the *Reliance*, the *Koyukuk*, and the *Delta*.

C. Waugaman Collection

During breakup in Fairbanks in 1911, the span on the bridge has been pulled back onto the banks to avoid its destruction. The pilings often were destroyed by the ice, however, and had to replaced annually.

C. Waugaman Collection

The woman in the background shows the relative size of ice during breakup on the Chena Slough in Fairbanks in 1911. The boats tied up in the background no doubt were protected from the ravages of the ice.

C. Waugaman Collection

The Graehl ferry was one of two that operated on the Chena Slough. This one was located at Cushman Street, and was put into service temporarily each spring when the ice destroyed the bridge pilings. Fees charged on the ferry were used to rebuild the bridge.

C. Waugaman Collection

At least eight steamboats can be seen in this photograph of the Fairbanks waterfront in 1913. This bridge was known as "The Christmas Tree Bridge" because of the trees on it.

Bunnell Collection, UAF archives

The sternwheeler *Hannah*, operated by the Northern Navigation Co., leaves Eagle on the Yukon River, circa 1904.

Chapter 1. Barnette and the *Lavelle Young*

In the late 1890s commerce became intense along the Upper Yukon and the U.S. government began planning improved access to Alaska. The first concern was for a trail between the coastal town of Valdez and Fort Egbert at Eagle on the Yukon. Trail construction began in 1901.[1]

John Jerome Healy, a railroad visionary, decided to build a railroad along the same route. This dream never materialized but a friend of his — E.T. Barnette — decided that the spot where this trail and the planned railroad would cross the Tanana River (Tanacross or Tanana Crossing) would be the ideal place to start a trading post. As Barnette envisioned it, this post would serve the entire Tanana Valley, as it was to be located halfway between Valdez and Eagle. It would be accessible in the summer by the Tanana River and have year-round connections via rail to the Yukon River and the deep sea port of Valdez.

Barnette went into partnership with Charles Smith in November 1900, then went to San Francisco and bought $20,000 worth of trading goods for his post. He arranged to have the supplies shipped to St. Michael the next summer. Then he was off to Circle City on the Yukon River where he paid $10,000 for the steamboat *Arctic Boy*. When the river opened he took her down to St. Michael to await his supplies.[2]

In St. Michael, before Barnette's supplies arrived, a crew member — or an entire crew, depending on the story you prefer — took the *Arctic Boy* out for a run and, being unfamiliar with the submerged rocks in the harbor, tore the bottom out of the boat. Desperate, Barnette persuaded Captain C.W. Adams, co-owner with Thomas Bruce of the *Lavelle Young*, to take him upstream. The *Lavelle Young* was a dredge boat at that time, built in or near Portland, Oregon, to come to the Koyukuk River to dredge for gold. That endeavor never panned out (literally or figuratively), so the boat was converted to a packet for carrying passengers and cargo.

Captain Adams knew of no one who had taken a steamboat up the Tanana River, but he had heard that above the Chena Slough was Bates Rapids which he surmised were impassable for a steamboat.[3] Captain Adams agreed to try to take Barnette to Tanacross, but he made it clear he could not guarantee success. Their agreement included one price to the Chena Slough and an additional price if they could go farther.

When the *Lavelle Young* headed upriver, E.T. Barnette and his wife were onboard along with three or four other men in Barnette's employ in addition to the usual crew and approximately 130 tons of supplies for Barnette's trading post. The cargo included general supplies, one horse, a team of dogs, windows and doors, a sled, a steam launch, tools, prospecting equipment, hardware and basic food.

They had no trouble on the Yukon, with which Captain Adams was quite familiar, and they successfully navigated the Lower Tanana. However, the Tanana was low in the fall of 1901, and they were unable to get past the Bates Rapids. Barnette suggested that they drop back to the Chena Slough, because he had heard from some Indians that the upper end of the slough branched from the Tanana River above the rapids.[4] This was true. The lower end of what we now call the Chena River was at that time the mouth of a sizable slough of the Tanana River. That slough left the Tanana some 40 miles above Fairbanks and rejoined it 10 miles below Fairbanks. Midway, what was then called the Big Chena River joined the Chena Slough. So, at that time, the waters of the Tanana River, possibly via what we now know as Moose Creek, fed into the Chena Slough and gave it far more volume than it has today.

Captain Ådams agreed to try the Chena Slough. However, before they had sounded their way half the length of the slough the water proved to be too low. The *Lavelle Young* had to stop. Captain Adams reminded Barnette that their agreement had been to let Barnette off at the farthest point they could reach. Barnette preferred to be taken back to the Tanana River. There, it would be easier for another boat — particularly one of shallower draft — to pick him up the following summer when the river was higher and take him the rest of the way to Tanacross. However, Captain Adams refused to take him and his gear back to the Tanana River. Going downstream with a full load, the *Lavelle Young* could lodge on a sand bar. With the current pushing from behind, it could have proven difficult to get free especially since the *Lavelle Young* did not have a steam winch or capstan to help pull herself off.

Adams and Barnette compromised, returning to a point eight or 10 miles from the mouth of the slough. There Captain Adams unloaded the Barnettes, their hired help and the trading post supplies. It was early fall, 1901.[5]

Chapter 2. The Founding of Fairbanks

The crew of the *Lavelle Young* helped unload the freight. They erected a shelter for the Barnette family to live in and to store the supplies. Then, without ceremony, Captain Adams shoved off for St. Michael.[1]

Although Barnette did not know it for another year, he could not have been let off at a better place. The *Lavelle Young's* inability to navigate the Bates Rapids or the upper portion of the Chena Slough placed him at the right place at the right time. Prospectors Felix Pedro (born Felice Pedroni) and Tom Gilmore were at that moment coming down out of the surrounding hills to investigate the smoke they had seen rising from the steamboat's stack. They had been about to head back to Circle for more supplies when they had seen the smoke and were delighted to find Barnette with supplies close at hand. By July of the following year, before Barnette would have a chance to bring in a shallower draft boat and move to Tanacross, Pedro would find gold and Fairbanks would be on its way.

However, the little camp that Barnette called Chenoa[2] City, but later named Fairbanks, was to have bitter competition in becoming the most important town in the Tanana Valley. That same year (1901) George Belt and Nathan Hendricks, as agents of the North American Transportation and Trading Company (N.A.T.&T.), were establishing a trading post on the Tanana River across from the mouth of the Chena Slough. They planned to trade with the Indians, and to sell supplies to the miners who were exploring the area and to men who were installing the telegraph lines down the Tanana River to Fort Gibbon.[3]

Barnette was dropped at the future site of Fairbanks toward the end of August. In September, the *Tanana Chief*, which in 1898 had carried 18 prospectors up the Chena Slough, towed a barge with 70 tons of supplies and building materials to the site of Hendricks' and Belt's post.[4] In the spring of 1902, the men moved across the river to the mouth of the Chena Slough where their post would become the town of Chena and an intense rival of Barnette's venture. Sometimes, the odds favored Chena and at other times, Fairbanks. After a decade of competition, Chena failed and today not even a ghost town remains.

During winter of 1901-1902, Barnette did some trading with the local Indians for furs, but spent a great deal of time making plans for the following summer. On March 10, 1902, he left his camp with his wife and three of the men to walk out to Valdez. They followed a trail that one of Barnette's men, Dan McCarty, had blazed earlier that winter. It took them about a month to cover the 400 miles to Valdez, with the temperatures sometimes reaching –40° F.[5] From there they went to Seattle, where Barnette bought additional supplies and a shallow-draft boat, which he named the *Isabelle*, after his wife.[6] He had the little steamer dismantled and shipped to St. Michael. There it was reassembled in the Northern Commercial Company's shipyard. The machinery from the sunken *Arctic Boy* was retrieved and installed in the *Isabelle*.[7]

Barnette was in St. Michael supervising the assembly of his boat when he met Judge James Wickersham. During this meeting Judge Wickersham suggested that Barnette name his future trading post Fairbanks, after Senator Charles W. Fairbanks — later to become vice president of the United States. Wickersham, in return, indicated that he would do what he could to help Barnette's venture.[8]

It was a deal that Barnette probably never had reason to regret, since Wickersham's help turned out to be influential in the development of Fairbanks as a permanent town. Wickersham, on the other hand, often had reason to regret his association with Barnette.

Barnette left St. Michael on the *Isabelle* in August 1902. He planned to return to the Chena Slough, load his supplies from the previous year and head up the Tanana River, conquer Bates Rapids and, hence, to Tanana Crossing. With him went a crew of eight, which probably included himself as captain. Mr. A.M. Thompson is listed as first officer, John E. Floyd as engineer, Matt Meehan as assistant engineer, Dan McCarty and Fred Noyes as firemen, Tom Larson as carpenter and Jujiro Wada (also known as "Wada the Jap") as cook.[9]

Barnette's plans were scuttled again, however, because the Tanana River and Chena Slough were even lower in September 1902 than they had been the previous year. This time, he could not even get his shallow-draft boat up the Chena Slough as far as the *Lavelle Young* had made it the year before and had to stop about four miles short of his previous camp. He knew if the *Isabelle* could get no farther up the Chena than that, he probably would not get past Bates Rapids that season.

It was at this time, however, that he learned of Felix Pedro's gold strike during the month of July — and immediately changed his plans. He rushed out with his crew members and started staking claims as fast as he could. Twenty-five to 30 men were staking claims in the general area of Pedro's strike. Within a few days they held a miners' meeting at which Barnette was elected temporary recorder for their claims, and he persuaded them to name his camp Fairbanks.[10]

Barnette was in a hurry to get Fairbanks established as the most important town in the Interior. To do that, he needed more miners bringing out gold so he spread the news of the Fairbanks strike far and wide — and the news he spread was sometimes far from the truth. He believed the gold was there, just as he had believed there would be no problem getting steamboats up the Tanana River to Tanana Crossing. When more miners did arrive, he figured the gold *would* start coming out of the ground in a big way and everybody would be happy. Thus he wrote many letters, salted a mine for a visitor,[11] and sent Jujiro Wada, the cook, to Dawson to talk up the discovery.[12]

Chapter 3. The Fairbanks Stampede

In December 1902 and January 1903 men began arriving from Rampart in response to the reports by the unknowing victim of the salted mine. And, when Wada finished spreading his embroidered story in Dawson, a stampede was in full swing.

But the stampeders found there was little wealth coming out. While it was true that this was rich gold-bearing ground, it was not gold that could be reached easily. It was buried deep, sometimes as deep as 180 feet.[1] A prospector began by building a fire on the frozen ground. He shoveled the thawed earth aside, then built another fire, thawing and digging until he hit bedrock. Miners averaged about a foot a day.

The best claims quickly were staked. Soon the mining district needed fewer men and more equipment. The miners wanted boilers with steampoints to increase the rate at which the ground could be thawed. And they wanted steam winches to haul the thawed overburden up from below when the holes got deep. This machinery took money. Investors were not yet convinced that the Fairbanks strike was worth the risk and the stampede slowed to a trot. Many who came were not miners but speculators. There was a range of people: businessmen, storekeepers, freighters, and a few professionals such as doctors and lawyers. There were debtors, gamblers, fortunetellers and dance hall girls.[2] By March 1903 the good claims had been staked. Late-comers were finding the only money to be had was the money they had brought with them. Food was becoming scarce.[3]

Veteran miners believed the gold would not be coming out of the ground in paying quantities for at least another year. By April, people were starting to leave Fairbanks. Some were hurrying for Dawson by dog team before the snow melted. Others had to wait for the ice to go out so they could leave by steamboat. The ice went out on May 7. Many, not wanting to wait several more weeks until a steamboat would come, built or bought small boats and floated down the Tanana River to the town of Tanana where they could meet a Yukon River steamer.[4]

The stampede was over and only about 400 people remained.[5] Since the gold was slow to come out of the prospect shafts, the majority of speculators and investors remained unconvinced that Fairbanks and Chena were good risks. Yet there were men who believed in the gold and believed in the future of one or the other of the towns.

Chapter 4. Fairbanks Settles Down

Fairbanks Weekly News, Local Happenings, September 19, 1903.

Enos Hansen has finished his residence on Wendel Avenue. John Ronan and Charles Oesterie, of 1 above, left limit of Cleary creek, were in town Tuesday. They have struck good pay, and will work the ground this winter with machinery.

A contract was let this week for the erection of a two-story hotel on the Butler & Gibson lot, just above the Commissioner's office, on First avenue. It is the intention of the owners to have a first class hostelry in every particular.

Between 20 and 30 buildings are in course of construction, and others are being started daily. Fairbanks is the largest log cabin town in the world today, and the number of buildings will be doubled by the first of the year. There are but few vacant buildings, those now under construction are not for rent, and the population of the town is rapidly increasing.

The river raised about six inches last night.

The FAIRBANKS NEWS office is prepared to fill any order for fine job printing. Send in your order.

Mrs. F.G. Noyes is expected to arrive on the Kuyokuk this evening from Seattle to spend the winter.

The Skagway Guide of a late date publishes the statement that the Jap, Wada, who is accused of stealing a lot of valuable furs from Capt. Barnette, had been apprehended there and taken into custody, and would be returned to Fairbanks for trial. Wada was employed as a cook by Capt. Barnette last winter, when he is supposed to have purloined the furs.

During the stampede of the previous winter, differences between Chena and Fairbanks began to emerge. Many of the stampeders came from Rampart, Tanana, and Glenn Gulch. They knew Hendricks and Belt from their other trading posts on the Yukon River, and tended to make the Chena trading post, now moved to the mouth of the Chena Slough, their headquarters. The men who hiked in overland from the upper Yukon River came to Fairbanks first and tended to settle there.

Less good land was available in Chena and there were fewer good trees for building material.[1] This led to claim-jumping, land speculation, and unrest. In Fairbanks, more land was available, plus a good supply of standing timber. Just as important, Barnette understood how to make a town grow by making land easily accessible. He staked only a 350′ x 350′ lot for his trading post. All surrounding lots were available for whomever wanted to stake them and pay a $2.50 recorder's fee.[2] Early in 1903, an effort was made to stake out the town lots and map blocks.[3]

Judge James Wickersham came to Fairbanks in April 1903. He described it as having eight cabins, a few tents, Barnette's trading post, and a partially furnished two-story building.[4] He was not disturbed by the apparent failure of the boom. He was one of the "true believers" and he went ahead with plans to transfer the mining claim recording office from Eagle to Fairbanks. In the next four years, 12,000 claims would be recorded in this office.[5] Obviously, miners continued coming to Fairbanks, though without the fanfare of a stampede.

By July there were four buildings on Garden Island across the Chena Slough from Fairbanks (See Map 3) and 22 buildings in Fairbanks itself.[6] (Fairbanks was on a large island, bounded by the Chena Slough on the north and the Tanana River on the south. (See Map 2) This is not true any longer with the drying up of the east end of the slough.) The residents were enthusiastic about their new town and applied to the District Court in Rampart to become a municipal government. The court could not act on this request immediately so the townspeople formed a government by consent.[7] Even though mining was slow, new businesses were starting. Two sawmills, a grocery store, a newspaper, and a machinery company all appeared by the end of that summer. The old, established Northern Commercial Company bought into Barnette's Trading Post.[8]

In May 1903, the first Fairbanks postmaster was commissioned. Mail was to be delivered 12 times a year by steamboat.[9] Barnette donated a parcel from his trading post site to the U.S. government for a courthouse and jail site.[10] Chena was connected to the telegraph system in Alaska in 1903 when the line was laid along the Tanana River. Through special request, Fairbanks was also linked, probably in early 1904.[11] By August 1905, a building in Fairbanks housed the U.S. Army Signal Corps.[12] In 1904, money originally intended to improve the road between Valdez and Eagle was reappropriated to build the 400-mile trail between Valdez and Fairbanks, the latter being recognized as the most important town in the Interior. This provided a route for winter mail delivery. By the winter of 1905-06, Fairbanks was the mail distribution center for the Interior, including Nome.[13]

As predicted, mining started to pick up during the summer of 1903. Two small steam boilers were used that summer and another two were being installed, thawing ground in the drifts at 400 cubic feet per day.[14] More miners had moved into the area — not the kind looking for a quick strike, but experienced men who understood placer mining. During August and September they washed their dirt piles and found enough gold to be encouraged. The six major creeks of the time produced a total of about $40,000 worth of gold that year.[15]

Then, in September, Dennis O'Shea struck it rich on "8 Above" on Moose Creek. He went to Hendricks' and Belt's post in Chena to ask for credit on provisions. The store sent someone out to the mine to check O'Shea's report. The story was true. They expected that news of this big strike would bring another stampede. Hendricks knew that neither he nor all of Fairbanks had enough supplies to feed a large number of people for the winter so he immediately sent a telegram to the North American Transportation and

Trading Company near Tanana requesting food shipments. E.W. Griffith, the agent there, diverted the freight of two steamboats, the *J.B. Powers* and the *John Hamilton*, to the Tanana Valley. Three more good strikes were made before the end of December. However, a section of the telegraph lines were down, owing to a forest fire. Moreover, people were leery of gold strike news coming from the Tanana Valley now and the newspapers gave the event little coverage.[16]

It probably was just as well that the news did not spread quickly, because Hendricks proved to be correct: There was a shortage of food in the valley. Some supplies could be hauled over the trails in the winter, but for all practical purposes steamboats were the only means of shipping sufficient quantities of food and supplies to the Interior towns and villages. It took time for an order for provisions to be sent out to Seattle. Then those provisions had to be assembled and loaded on an ocean-going vessel for Alaska.

There were two main access routes for freight to the Interior. One was via ocean liner to Skagway where a train connected to Whitehorse in Yukon Territory, Canada. From Whitehorse, steamboats carried the merchandise downstream to Dawson and on to Tanana, Weare or Ft. Gibbon, all close to the junction of the Tanana and Yukon rivers. Either that boat or another one then came up the Tanana River to the Chena Slough and to Fairbanks. This route, only 2,375 miles, was the shortest according to the *Fairbanks, Alaska Survey of Progress*, but it was also the most expensive and involved two customs checks before arrival.[17]

The other route was from Seattle to St. Michael on the west coast of Alaska. Because the mouth of the Yukon River was spread over such a large area, it was shallow, and boats with a draft of more than three or four feet could not get through. Freight and passengers were off-loaded at St. Michael (and sometimes Nome) to another steamboat for the run up the Yukon.[18] If the destination was Fairbanks, the goods again were transferred at Tanana (or Weare or Ft. Gibbon) to a boat that was going up the Tanana. This route took longer (close to 4,000 miles and as long as six weeks),[19] but it was cheaper and involved no customs checks.[20]

Orders had to be sent out in the spring or early summer for provisions to arrive before the rivers got too shallow or frozen in the fall. In the spring and early summer of 1903, with most of the stampeders gone or trying to leave, the merchants had not placed large orders. Not until late in the summer did anyone realize that there were now considerably more miners in the district than had been anticipated in the early summer. The situation was made even more crucial with O'Shea's strike. The water was low in the Yukon and Tanana rivers again that year. That meant freight had to be changed to shallower draft boats at Tanana — a time-consuming operation when there was no time to spare. The smaller boats were hurrying back and forth frantically between the Chena and Fairbanks stores and Tanana.[21]

The first issue of the *Fairbanks Weekly News*, published September 19, 1903, reported several boats on their way or recently arrived at Fairbanks or Chena. The 450-ton steamer *John J. Healy* had landed the previous Wednesday with 75 tons of freight, five passengers and some mail. The *Healy* also was trying to bring up another 180 tons of provisions (part aboard the boat itself and part on a barge) before the end of the navigation season. Barnette's *Isabelle* had arrived on Wednesday with a full cargo of merchandise and 20 passengers. She left on Saturday for another load and hoped to be back by Monday or Tuesday. If there was time, she would try to make one more trip after that. Merchants hoped that between the *Isabelle* and *Kuyokuk*, another 300 tons of supplies would be delivered to Fairbanks. The *Kuyokuk* was to arrive on Monday with freight and passengers and it was planned that she would make one or two more trips. The *Tanana Chief*, the same boat that had come up the Chena Slough in 1898, was expected at Chena the next day with a full cargo of freight and a loaded barge.[22]

But winter came early that year and all the boats were frozen into the Yukon River. Two hundred people departed on the last boat out of town, but about 900 settled in for the Fairbanks winter.[23] Two refrigerator steamboats, the *Robert Kerr* and *J.P. Light*, with meat intended for Dawson, were among the stranded supply boats. Because of the crucial food situation, a portion of this meat was sledded to

Fairbanks during the winter.[24] A plentiful supply of rabbits, moose and caribou plus the general resourcefulness of the people kept the populations from starving, even though there was little variety in their diet.

Chapter 5. The Rise of Steamboating

According to the April 16, 1904, issue of *The Fairbanks Weekly News,* Barnette's company (now two-thirds owned by the N.C. Co.) had made plans to deal with the low water in the Chena Slough. "Neither *Tanana* nor *Koyukuk* will run to Gibbon. They will run only to what is known as the Lavelle Young Slough, about 40 miles below Fairbanks. There the Company would keep a floating warehouse consisting of a very large scow. These two boats will ply from the slough here constantly and with plenty of help, loading and unloading, it is expected that the round trip will be made within twenty-four hours. The scow will be supplied with freight by the *Rock Island* and *Seattle No. 3* and if required, the *Leah*, all of whom are to push barges from Gibbon to the slough...." They also announced that the *Koyukuk's* first trip of the season would be to Bettles on the Koyukuk River and then it would start its business in Fairbanks. Already by 1904 the town was beginning to concern itself not only with supplying itself, but also with supplying other mining camps that developed along or off the Tanana River and even the Yukon River.

The same issue of the *Fairbanks Weekly News* mentioned a William Waechter who had decided to build a dock and a two-story warehouse on the waterfront between the Mageau Building and the sawmill. He expected his first steamboat shipment of beef cattle to reach the town about the middle of June.[1]

That issue also described plans to extract the barge *Otter* and the steamboat *Isabelle* from the ice where they had spent the winter. A passage was to be cut in the ice along the shoreline to ease the boats along to an eddy where they would be safe during breakup.

Competition for the Fairbanks market among transportation companies was fierce. James H. Rogers, general agent for the White Pass Railway Company, was coming to Fairbanks in early August 1904, "to look over the field with a view to competing with the lower river boats for the transportation business of this camp."[2] This competition would remain as long as the steamboat was the source of supplies in town.

Most of the people's thoughts that spring of 1904, however, were on the arrival of the first boat of the season. Both the Fairbanks *Rock Island* and the *Lavelle Young* planned to be the earliest boats to bring freight to Fairbanks. The *Rock Island* was scheduled to bring 300 tons of supplies which had been shipped over the White Pass. The *Rock Island* and the *Lavelle Young* then would ply the Yukon and Tanana rivers until the freight had been cleared up.[3] On May 21 the first boat for Fairbanks left Dawson with 150 passengers and 300 tons of freight: livestock, whiskey, potatoes, beer and wagons. Two other heavily loaded boats soon followed.[4]

When the first boat of the 1904 season tied up at the dock at Fairbanks after the long winter without much food, goods were sold before they were off the boat. Eggs brought $50 per case.[5] The arrival of the first boat, especially the first boat with fresh perishables, was always a big event.

We know of only two editions of *The Fairbanks Weekly News* from the summer of 1904, but the July 30 issue tells a lot about the boats and the freight that came into the town that season. Palmer and Field, a store on Second Avenue in the old Arctic Brotherhood Hall, advertises "Just from the Outside: oranges, lemons, bananas and apples. New shipments on every steamer." Another store, Solly's, has in stock "chocolates, bon bons, tobacco of all kinds, good stationery and all kinds of magazines and papers."

And more of everything arrived on every steamboat. The *Koyukuk* had reached Fairbanks on the previous Wednesday, returning from a trip up the Koyukuk River to Bettles, one of the newest mining camps. Captain Boernier had taken the sternwheeler up the Koyukuk with a large list of passengers and all the freight she could handle. (Bettles ordered its supplies from Fairbanks even though Tanana and Weare were closer. We surmise that the miners in Bettles had stampeded from Fairbanks and felt an affinity for the place from which they had come.) The *Florence S.* arrived on Thursday with 50 tons of freight and 40 passengers. Her master, W.E. Warren, indicated that she would run between Ft. Gibbon and Fairbanks for the rest of the season.

The *Cudahy*, with Captain Holchier in charge, landed at Chena with 250 tons of freight and 45 passengers for Fairbanks. At 819 tons, the *Cudahy* was one of the largest sternwheelers of the day and one of the fastest at the time in the N.A.T.& T. fleet. The decision not to try to come up Chena Slough to Fairbanks was probably due to her size and the stage of the water.

The *Rock Island* was leaving soon to go down the Tanana River and the *Koyukuk* was heading up the Tanana River to take some prospectors to points along the river. The *Lavelle Young* was scheduled to pick up passengers from Dawson coming down the Yukon on the *Susie*.

The town was excited about the arrival of the new N.N.C. boat, the *Tanana*. Built earlier that spring in Portland, Oregon, at a cost of $40,000, she was shipped "knocked-down" to St. Michael to be reassembled. The *Tanana* was said to be "probably the fastest and most powerful light draught boat in the Yukon waters."[6] With a carrying capacity of 225 tons, she could accommodate 150 passengers and was so modern that she had electric cabin lights and electric search lights. As incredible as the figures seem, on this, her first trip from St. Michael to Fairbanks, with Captain James S. Grey as master, she is reported to have set a record of seven and a half days, with actual running time logged at five days and 17 hours. She had churned from Ft. Gibbon to Fairbanks in 17 hours. During spring breakup the following year the *Tanana* was in Fairbanks, tied up at the N.C. Co. dock. The flood swept a mass of ice and sawed logs downstream carrying the Wendell Street Bridge with it. Taking in the impending disaster at a glance, Captain McMann cast the *Tanana* loose and rode his boat downstream amidst the logs.[7]

Many issues of the *Fairbanks Evening News* from the 1905 shipping season still exist. From them we can assemble a clear picture of the steamboat commerce coming into Fairbanks that year, reflecting the lifestyle of the day. On August 3, Barrett Mercantile Co. advertises just off the *Lavelle Young* "the entire stock of Carlson and Deruchin, fresh beef & mutton, spring chickens, fruit and vegetables galore. Everything guaranteed fresh."[8] The beef and mutton were fresh; the animals were shipped alive and butchered after arrival. (Occasionally, livestock was also herded over the trail from Valdez.) Barnette's next days' ad proclaims that it has new goods coming weekly and that they now have in stock food, hay and oats.[9] Brumbaugh, Hamilton, and Kellog advertise 40 tons of stock including "New goods, Miners supplies, Hardware, Graniteware, Tinware."[10] Another store lists "fresh ham and bacon, butter in pickle [brine], eggs, potatoes, onions, cheese, oranges, lemons, canned vegetables, etc."[11]

Fairbanks Evening News, July 18, 1905

TO ITALY FOR BRIDE

> *Felix Pedro Sails for the Outside. After an Old Sweetheart.*
>
> *Felix Pedro, the well known pioneer of the Tanana is on his way to Italy to get a bride. He was a passenger on the Tanana sailing last evening for the connecting boats for the outside.*
>
> *Mr. Pedro told a friend that the American girls were all right and that the fairest of the fair were residents of Fairbanks, but that he wanted one of his own countrywomen. In fact, he has in mind, so it is said a black-eyed Italian girl with whom he parted in the sunny southland years ago when he turned his steps toward America to make his fortune.*

The July 18, 1905, *Fairbanks Evening News* reports that the *Schwatka* was lying at Chena and her owner, C.W. Thebo, planned to winter her over in Lake LaBerge and bring her first load of 1906 to Fairbanks. Another article notes that the *Tanana* had left the evening before with a number of passengers; they would transfer at Tanana to other boats bound for St. Michael and Dawson.

Fairbanks Evening News, August 1, 1906

> *FINE SADDLE HORSE*
>
> *Brought here from Dawson for use of Mrs. Magaw.*
>
> *On the last steamer was a fine buggy and saddle horse for Mrs. C.A. Magaw. It came from Dawson and is the counterpart of the blooded horse owned by Captain Barnette. In fact, the two horses were matched and driven together in Dawson. They are not related, but it is scarcely possible to tell them apart. A discussion arose as to whether the horses would recognize each other when they met after their long separation. It is intended to have them meet as soon as possible and observe their actions.*

The August 1 issue says that the *Healy* and *Weare* were due to arrive Thursday with large cargoes of freight and some passengers. The *Cudahy* was due to arrive the next day with 200 tons of railroad iron (presumably for the Tanana Mines Railroad), and she would leave the next Thursday for St. Michael to connect with boats going Outside.

That edition of the *Fairbanks Evening News* also mentions that the 293-ton *Delta* was departing August 2 for her first trip up the Tanana River. Like the *Tanana* she was a sternwheeler similar to the *Koyukuk* but smaller. She evidently had been built that year (1905) in Portland, Oregon, for reassembly in St. Michael. Her officers for that summer were:

Captain S.B. Short; Captain A.W. Grey (brother of the *Tanana's* Captain Grey); First Officer: Nelson Delude; Purser: R. Fulcher; Chief Engineer: George Kenney; Second Engineer: Halpen.

On her first trip from St. Michael to Fairbanks, the *Delta* brought 90 tons of freight. According to the August 4 issue of the paper, when she left for the Upper Tanana she was "loaded to the guards with freight and passengers."[12]

The N.A.T.& T. Company's *Cudahy* sailed the morning of August 4 for St. Michael with passengers for Nome and Seattle. The *Power* had left Dawson with 200 tons of railroad material for the Tanana Mines Railroad. The *Weare* headed downstream from Chena the day before for Ft. Gibbon to connect with the *Isom*. And the *Healy* began pushing upriver from Ft. Gibbon the night before with a full cargo of freight for Fairbanks.

The August 7 issue reports that the *Ella* had returned from taking 40 tons of provisions up the Tanana River to the Nabesna River, 50 miles or more beyond Barnette's original goal of Tanacross. This may have been the run on which *Ella* earned the distinction of traveling farther up the Tanana than any steamboat had traveled. On the 7th the *Rock Island* was to steam out with passengers, including E.T. Barnette, his wife and their child and her nurse, to make connections for the Outside. That edition also reports a new independent steamer line that had been launched by Captain Calderhead to compete with the other two major lines. It does not state the name of the new company but it does list the boats and their freight tonnage which evidently belonged to or perhaps were leased by the new company. The list also included the planned itineraries of each boat.

NAME OF BOAT	TONNAGE	INTENDED PLACES
Minneapolis	100 tons	St. Michael-Fairbanks
Wilbur Crimmin	150 tons (with barge)	Tanana River
Helen Bruce	20 tons	Fairbanks-Chena
Dusty Diamond	50 tons	Ft. Gibbon-Chena
Laura	light draft tributaries	Tanana River and
Florence S.	30 tons	Lower Tanana River
Luella	60 tons	Tanana River
Schwatka	200 tons	St. Michael, Fairbanks, Whitehorse
J.P. Light	400 tons	St. Michael, Fairbanks, Dawson
Tanana Chief	20 tons	Lower Tanana River
Little Delta	20 tons	Tanana River/ tributary
Ella	75 tons	Fairbanks/Tanana Crossing

Calderhead's company planned round trips between Ft. Gibbon and Fairbanks in seven days including loading and unloading; they hoped to move close to 5,000 tons a month. The N.A.T.& T. in the same newspaper listed the following boats: *Isom, Power, Cudahy, Weare, Healy, Hamilton,* and the *John Barr.*

On August 9, the *Fairbanks Evening News* stated that the *White Seal* had returned the previous day from the Kantishna River and that the *Margaret* was due in the next day. On the 12th, it was reported that the *Ella* had been bought by Bishoprick and Bain. Under their ownership, she would make one or two more trips to St. Michael, then might be assigned to the Kantishna. On the 15th, the *Tana, Florence S.* and the *Luella* all fired up their boilers for the Kantishna River. The *Tanana,* meanwhile, was ready to depart for Tanana with passengers going Outside. Ten days later, the *Tanana* was due in the evening with mail, passengers and "considerable through freight." The *Rock Island* arrived the previous night with passengers. The furor to get to the Kantishna leaves little doubt that a new gold strike, and with it a new mining camp, had been reported down the river.

The September 13 *Fairbanks Evening News* announced that a special train was to run from Fairbanks to Chena, taking passengers to the *John S. Cudahy* the following day for departure to Ft. Gibbon. The *Weare* had arrived at Chena the previous afternoon and the *Margaret* had docked in Fairbanks in the evening. The *Tanana* reached Fairbanks that afternoon with mail and passengers. The *Ella* arrived the same day in the late morning. The *Minneapolis* would be leaving on the 14th for various points along the Kantishna River, with plenty of room for freight and passengers. The advertisement warned that the shipping season was nearly over. By September 23, the steamboats hurried to get the freight cleaned up before the season ended. The *Tanana* hauled for Ft. Gibbon on that day. The *Cudahy,* with a Captain Dobler as master, also departed and was to winter over at St. Michael. The *Koyukuk* and *Delta* were at Fairbanks, the *Rock Island* and the *Monarch* were due to arrive the next day, and the *Florence S.* and the *Schwatka* would be in that afternoon. The *Isom* was on her way with 100 passengers for Fairbanks and then intended to winter over at St. Michael. The *Healy* also intended to spend the winter at St. Michael, while the *Weare* and the *Power* would winter at Dawson.

The last available edition of the paper for the 1905 steamboating season is September 25. According to that issue, the steamer *John J. Healy* would leave the next day to connect with the *Power* at Gibbon. Passengers from Fairbanks would ride to Chena on the 10:00 a.m. train. The *Campbell, Schwatka,* and *Healy* were at Chena; the *Rock Island* and *Weare* were due, and the *Monarch* was overdue at Chena. The *Tanana* was heading for Dawson the next day while the *Schwatka* would leave for the same place on the 28th.

Chapter 6. Fairbanks Grows

Fairbanks Evening News, July 30, 1903

The regular meeting of the town council was called to order at 8 o'clock Tuesday evening. Aldermen Spring, Petree, Smith, Sherman and Hall present. Mayor Barnette being absent from town Alderman Hall was appointed acting mayor.

The School Board submitted the contract engaging Miss Florence Heilig as teacher for a term of eight months from Sept. 12 to May 12. The salary of the teacher was agreed upon to be $175 per month, payable monthly. An understanding was also reached between the council and the school board that the latter body would incur no further indebtedness than would be covered by one third of the city's income as provided by an order of the court under the old statute.

The report of the municipal magistrate for the month of July showed that the sum of $1,050 had been collected for fines and infractions. The town treasurer acknowledged receipt of same.

The report of the poll tax collectors showed that only $452.00 had been collected to date.

The following bills were present by Town Clerk Badger and having been certified by various committees, were ordered and paid:

Carroll & Parker $86.00
A.A. Turnbarge, work on sidewalks 22.50
Tanana Dev. Co., building material 106.00
E. Wickersham, town constable 165.00
Boston Clothing House. 5.00
Abe Spring, city attorney 109.00

John Ginvin, repairs to pump 12.00
Wm. Poschke, marshal's badge 10.00
J.H. Heath, repairs on Cushman 69.00

Food supplies were short during the winter of 1903-04, but Fairbanksans still had time for civic issues and social events. According to the *Fairbanks Weekly News,* of September 19, 1903, there were about 400 houses in the community at that time. Fairbanksans voted to become a municipal government in November and the town was incorporated on December 26, with Barnette as its first mayor.[1]

The council was busy planning for sidewalks, drains, fire protection, water power, lights and schools. On November 7, the Arctic Brotherhood, a fraternal order, held a "smoker" at its lodge with over 250 in attendance. A phonograph with a large horn and a six-piece orchestra entertained the guests.[2] On Thanksgiving Day, the members held a by-invitation-only gathering at their lodge with 66 men and 17 women invited.[3]

During early fall, Fairbanks received the mail via dog team service along the Yukon River. However, during the winter a mail route was started from Valdez to Tanana. This route utilized a military road as far as the mouth of the Delta River, then followed the Tanana River to Fairbanks, and on to Tanana. This was about 10 days quicker than by the Yukon River and served well when the riverboat season closed.[4]

The news of O'Shea's find and the other strikes continued to spread slowly. People made their way to Fairbanks in the winter (bringing their own food supplies with them) and in greater numbers during the summer. During the years of 1905 and 1906, Fairbanks probably grew at its fastest rate. From about 900 people in the fall of 1903, the population rose to 3,000 in the district in 1904 and to 6,000 by the summer of 1905. Gold was the pacemaker: $40,000 was produced in 1903; $400,000 was taken out in 1904, and $600,000 in 1905. It was close to its peak in 1906 at $9,320,000.[5]

The Fairbanks businessmen were busy providing the services and amenities that would make the inhabitants happy. At first, a cable ferry transported men and supplies over Chena Slough to the trails that led toward the mines. In 1904, the Fairbanks City Council gave permission to Archie Burns to build a 305-foot bridge at Cushman Street and First Avenue over to Garden Island. It was to have a 40-foot drawbridge for steamboat traffic. The bridge was built in 1904 or 1905.[6] Another bridge at Wendell Street was built at about the same time.

After both the Wendell Street and Cushman Street bridges were lost to ice in 1905, the Turner Street bridge was built. This bridge was also built as a drawbridge. The draw was very cumbersome and seldom used except to save the bridge during breakup each year. An article in the June 8, 1910, *Fairbanks Daily News Miner* reported that the "home-built steamer *Little Snug* spent most of the day up against the Turner Street bridge waiting for the bridge to open and let her through."

Every spring when the ice was about to go out, men stood watch, then manually pulled the span back. Then only the pilings were damaged by the surge of ice. After breakup was over they would haul out the pile driver, put in new pilings and replace the span. Until the new pilings were in, the old cable ferry served. The fees for riding the ferry were used to pay for repairs to the bridge. After 1913, the cumbersome drawspan of the bridge was eliminated. This awkward situation of replacing the bridge prevailed every year until the Alaska Road Commission built an all-steel bridge in 1917 at Cushman Street.[7] It was not built as a drawbridge because the foot of Cushman Street marked the "head of navigation on the Chena River, but it will be high enough above the water to permit motor boats and other small craft to go under it." At high water the bridge was designed to be 12 feet above the water level, and at low water, 17 feet.[8]

In 1904, the businessmen took up a subscription to build a road to the mining camps. The trails were terrible in the summer, making it costly to get equipment through. To freight equipment to Cleary Creek, 22 miles from Fairbanks, cost up to $15 per pound. It only cost $2.50 per pound in the winter after freeze-up.[9] Once the miners started retrieving the gold from their winter piles, they also contributed to the fund. By May, $3,000 had been raised and with that amount, 13 miles of road were built. Teamsters had cooperated and hauled the materials free.[10]

First Avenue businesses now included 10 saloons and about the same number of restaurants. On Cushman Street resided a steam laundry, two meat markets, a dry goods store, a jewelry store, a wallpaper and paint store, and various other businesses. The N.C. Co. had two warehouses and a light and power plant. A 75-horsepower engine lit 1,000 lights in Fairbanks. The N.C. Co. facilities were located on the Garden Island side of the Chena Slough. Across the river on the Fairbanks side was the N.C. dock. Close by was the Pioneer Hotel, and adjacent to that was its Pioneer dock. One or two small docks also occupied the waterfront.[11] Two lumber mills were producing 25,000 board feet per day in the summer of 1905 and even that wasn't enough.[12] Phones were installed in Fairbanks and soon were ringing in the camps as well. Judge Wickersham designated the town as the headquarters for the Third (later to become the Fourth) Judicial District of Alaska.[13]

By 1906, water supply systems and fire mains served the town.[14] People also were discovering that they were able to grow gardens despite their far-north location. As early as 1904, they requested an agriculture station. It was started in 1907.[15]

Another important change was that Fairbanks was becoming a family town. In 1904, the public records show 14 marriages and four births, whereas the 1903 records show none.[16] By the end of September 1904, there were three churches (St. Matthew's Episcopal, Presbyterian, and Catholic), and one hospital (St. Matthew's) with accommodations for 16 patients.[17] Families required a different type of goods. Stores began selling household furnishings, fixtures, and necessities for homes and businesses. Women appeared at social events wearing gowns from New York and Paris.[18] The City Council made a five-month contract for a school between January and May of 1904. A disagreement between the School Board and City Council caused a relatively long interruption, but during the 1904-05 school year a full session was held.[19]

Fairbanks Evening News, May 7, 1904

Public School Closes. The Fairbanks public school closed yesterday. The following are the pupils who attended and the number of days attendance during this term.

Fiuan Delaney, 70; Eva Delaney, 60; Helen Lunbocker, 71; Richard Lunbocker, 70; Mary Harrington, 65; Catherine Harrington, 42; May Watson, 60; Madaline Nicholi, 40; Margarette Petree, 60.

Those who attended the closing exercises were Mrs. Kellum, Mrs. McChesney, Judge Wickersham, Mr. H.J. Miller and Mr. Lunbocker.

During this period, the town of Chena also was making her bid to be the leading town in the Tanana Valley. Backed up against a ridge, Chena had the better building site, better water supply and, being on the Tanana River instead of the Chena, had the advantage as a river port. On the other hand, Chena's land prices were excessive, and materials for the mining camps had a longer trek overland from Chena than from Fairbanks.

Fairbanks Evening News, August 3, 1905

Baseball Game Next Sunday. Fairbanks fans are Aroused and Are Clearing Grounds and Getting Team Together. The baseball fans of Fairbanks do not intend that Chena shall have the chance to boast about having won the most games for the season, and have arranged another game to be played on the Fairbanks grounds next Sunday at 3:30 o'clock.

A formal challenge has been sent to the Chena team and has been accepted. The new grounds are being put in shape, and will be ready by the time the game is called. The railroad will make a special excursion rate for the benefit of the Chena people, the train leaving that place at 1 o'clock and returning will leave Fairbanks at 8 o'clock.

Fairbanks, as the center of law, order, and public records for the valley, attracted many people, but perhaps most important was the progressive attitude of the people who lived in Fairbanks.[20] For instance, low water in the Chena Slough was a problem for steamboats coming up to Fairbanks so the townspeople raised $12,000 to divert more water from the Tanana River directly into the Chena Slough.[21] Although not particularly successful, the effort shows the positive attitude of the people.

The final shift that made Fairbanks the leading transportation center in the Interior came from an unexpected source — the town of Chena itself.

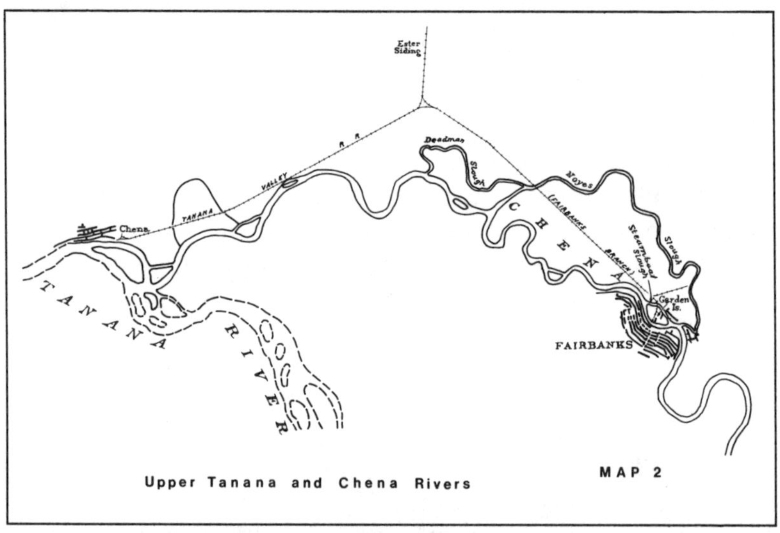

Upper Tanana and Chena Rivers

IN 1904, BUSINESS INTERESTS from Dawson City, Yukon Territory, decided to build a railroad from the town of Chena to carry heavy equipment and supplies to gold mines north of the city.

Backers of the Tanana Mines Railroad, later renamed the Tanana Valley Railroad, intended to lay the tracks straight to the mines from Chena without a cutoff to Fairbanks because the latter was more difficult than Chena to reach by steamboat.

However, when Falcon Joslin, who conceived the railroad, arrived in Interior Alaska, he wisely decided that a spurline to Fairbankswas needed. In all 45 miles were built, including the sections seen in this map.

Chapter 7. The First Railroad

Fairbanks Evening News, August 4, 1905

TANANA MINES RAILROAD CO.

Schedule of Trains

Until further notice trains will run as follows:

No. 1 — Leave Chena Daily . . . . 8:00 a.m.
Arrives Fairbanks . . . . 8:40 a.m.
No. 2 — Leaves Fairbanks . . . . 11:00 a.m.
Arrives Chena . . . . 11:40 a.m.
No. 3 — Leaves Chena . . . . 3:00 p.m.
Arrives Fairbanks . . . . 3:40 p.m.
No. 4 — Leaves Fairbanks . . . . 5:00 p.m.
Arrives Chena . . . . 5:40 p.m.

The company reserves the right to change this schedule at any time without notice.

C. Moriarity, Supt.; J.H. Scott, Gen. Agt.; Falcon Joslin, V.P. & G. Mgr.

A group of men came to Chena from Dawson to build a railroad to solve the problem of high transportation costs to the mines. Freight still was too expensive despite the new road, especially now that miners were bringing larger steam boilers to speed up the process of getting the gold out of the ground. A five horsepower steam boiler cost $500 in Fairbanks, but it could cost another $325 to move it to a claim just 25 miles away. A large 50 horsepower boiler that cost $3,000 in Fairbanks would cost another $3,000 to haul it to the mines — if the freighters could even haul it over the trails.[1] The success of the mining operations partly depended on being able to get the equipment to the mines inexpensively. And the success of Fairbanks depended on the success of the miners.

To solve that problem, the Tanana Mines Railroad (later to be called the Tanana Valley Railroad) was organized in 1904. The original plans were to go straight from Chena to the mines without a cutoff to Fairbanks. The thinking was that Chena was the natural head of navigation on the Tanana River, because when the water was low, the boats could only get up the Chena Slough with great difficulty, if at all. Therefore, Chena would be the logical place to start the rails. It also was thought that Fairbanks would soon go the way of most boom towns. However, when Falcon Joslin, the man behind the plan, came and viewed the situation himself, he decided that a spurline should be built to Fairbanks. He said it was because it would prevent another railroad from competing.[2] Possibly he was not convinced that Chena would survive; when it came time to build his home, he built it in Fairbanks.[3]

The railroad equipment arrived on the last boats of the 1904 season after being trans-shipped 11 times between Seattle and Chena. The spur to Fairbanks and the 26 miles of track to Gilmore were completed and were dedicated in a ceremony on July 17, 1905. Eventually, a total of 45 miles of track were laid.[4] The freight rates were, indeed, much lower. They started out at $.86 per ton per mile for freight and $.13 per mile for passengers. By 1908, the freight rate had dropped to $.58 per ton per mile.[5] By 1907 the *Directory of the Tanana Valley* reported that the Tanana Mine Railroad had paid all of its expenses and all of the improvements to date.

Fairbanksans were not overjoyed about these railroad plans at first and the beginning of the navigation season in 1904 caused them even more worry. The water was low again and the steamboats could not get up the slough to Fairbanks because of sandbars. A "mosquito fleet" of small, shallow-draft boats including the *Isabelle* scuttled back and forth bringing cargo and passengers from Chena to Fairbanks.[6] On some occasions during low water, horses would be used to carry the freight to Fairbanks.[7] (We can find no evidence — as has been suggested to us — that there were tow paths along which horses or mules pulled the boats. Evidently the paths that were reported along the Chena Slough were paths over which people and animals could walk, either carrying freight or transporting themselves.)

It was the railroad — which Fairbanksans originally had feared would detract from their town as the transportation center — that guaranteed its success. The railroad kept the people and the freight coming to Fairbanks even when the water was low. It kept them coming so well, indeed, that by 1907 Chena was on the decline with a population of about 450, while Fairbanks had at least 5,000.[8] Chena had become no more than a transfer point for freight on its way to Fairbanks. If the water was high enough the boats came on through; if not, the freight was transferred to the railroad cars at Chena, then sent to Fairbanks. In 1917, Chena virtually was abandoned and by 1920, the tracks between Chena and Fairbanks were torn up.[9] The headquarters of the railroad long since had been transferred from Chena to Garden Island across the river from Fairbanks.[10]

As important as the railroad was to the continuing growth of Fairbanks in the early years, we must underscore the point that the railroad could not have been built and would have had no purpose without the riverboats.

Virtually all the people, and all of their goods and possessions which contributed to the rapid growth of Fairbanks in these early years, came on the sternwheelers. This was well understood in that time and the ins and outs of steamboats affected most Fairbanksans' daily lives and plans.

Chapter 8. The Establishment of the Companies

With few trails and no roads, the rivers were the primary means of transportation. From the beginning of the exploration of the Interior, steamboats had been recognized as an important factor. In 1892 the North American Transportation and Trading Company (N.A.T.& T.) was organized in Chicago to compete in the Interior with the Alaska Commercial Company (A.C.C.).[1] In 1900 the A.C.C., the Seattle-Yukon Transportation Company, the Alaska Exploration Company and the Empire Line combined their businesses on the Yukon River to form the Northern Commercial Company. The "N.C. Co.," as it was known, concentrated on the trading and mercantile business, while its subsidiary, the Northern Navigation Company, (N.N.C.) dealt in the business of transportation. Thus, by the early 1900s there were two major transportation companies, the N.A.T.& T. and the N.N.C. These two had a virtual monopoly on the riverboat trade with little competition from independent steamers. The Pacific Cold Storage Company ran refrigerated steamboats to supply its plants on the Yukon with meat.[2] The N.A.T.& T. trading post was located at Weare and an early A.C.C. post was located at Tanana. By 1905, the N.N.C. had grown to 11 passenger and freight steamers, with a total freight capacity of 2,800 tons. These boats included the *Tanana*, the *Rock Island,* the *Lavelle Young,* the *Isabelle,* and the *Seattle No. 3*.[3] All came up the Tanana River to Fairbanks at one time or another.

Vital as the steamboats were, they were hampered severely in the Interior by the limited navigation season.

Chena Slough and the Tanana River opened relatively early — from April 29 to May 13 between 1903 and 1923[4]; May 12, 1920, and April 18, 1923. They usually closed by the end of the first week in October owing to ice or low water. This was a short season, but breakup of ice at the head and the mouth of the Yukon River was even later. The first steamer usually could not leave Whitehorse until mid-June. The last boat bound for Whitehorse or St. Michael had to leave Fairbanks by October 1 most years.[5] The Tanana Valley often would not receive supplies from outside of Alaska until mid- or late-June from Whitehorse and mid- or late-July via St. Michael.

However, as the steamboat companies gained experience with the short shipping season, they began wintering boats at Dawson, instead of Whitehorse. If the ice was late in going out of Lake Laberge, or if a downriver community was short of necessities, a boat could be sent out to relieve these communities (providing Dawson had the "shorts"; or they could be sledded over Lake Laberge from the freight stockpiled on the other side.)

Merchants' predictions as to the needs of their community were crucial and had to be made months in advance. If they guessed wrong, they could run short as happened in 1903-04, or they could find an unsold surplus on their shelves in the spring.

Sidney Paige, a writer for the *National Geographic,* in 1905 wrote of his experiences traveling on steamboats from Whitehorse to Fairbanks. The first boats to leave Whitehorse in the summer and the last few in the fall heading back to Whitehorse were often crowded, with room for "standees" only. Paige described a first-class ticket on a first-class steamer as getting a stateroom if you were lucky and sleeping under a table if you were not. A second-class ticket on a first-class boat allowed you a space above the boiler or on the bow. First- and second-class tickets on a second-class boat evoked thoughts of "if I'd only stayed to home with mother." He added that the wise and independent traveled on open boats.[6]

As unpredictable as the steamboat lifeline was, nearly everything that came to Fairbanks in the first 15 or 20 years came on the steamboats — from eggs to automobiles. Ironically, steamboats eventually carried their own death knell — the rails and cars for the Alaska Railroad, which would supply faster, cheaper and year-round service to the Interior.

PART II: Early Fairbanks' Peak Years (1906-1909)

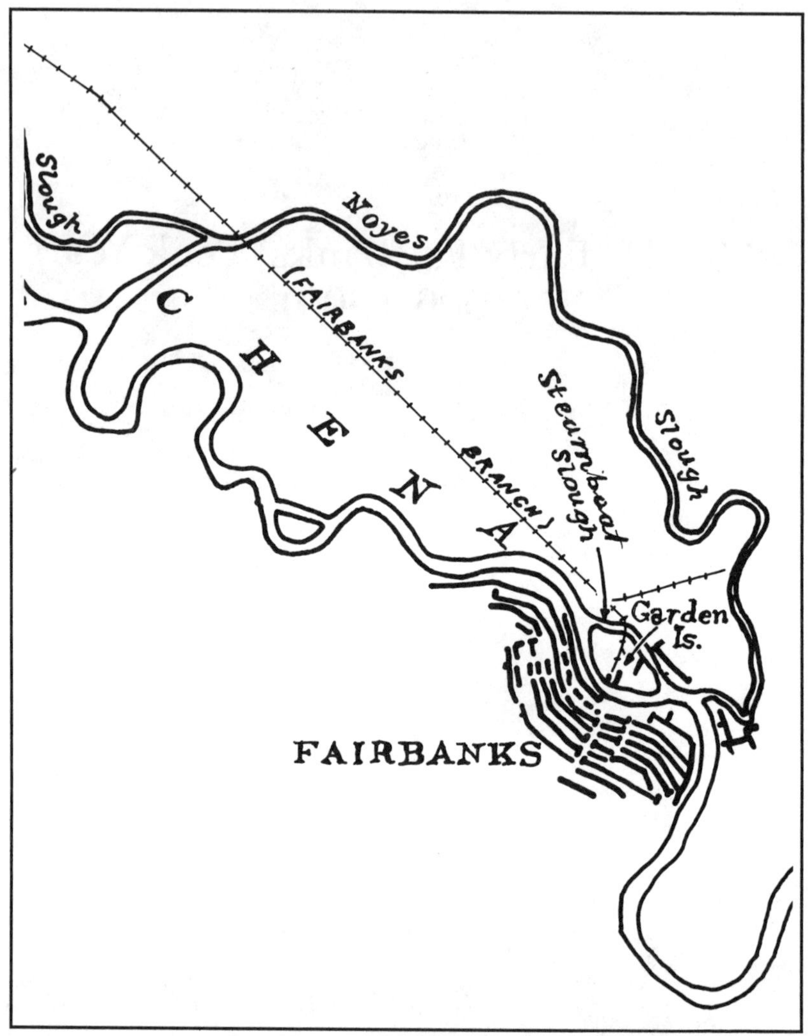

STEAMBOAT SLOUGH AND GARDEN ISLAND are important features on this map of early Fairbanks. Steamboats wintering over at Fairbanks often were pulled into sloughs, or pulled out of the water altogether, to avoid ice damage from breakup the following spring.

The unpredictability of freeze-up and low water sometimes left boats stranded. In the fall of 1906, the crew of the *Portus B. Weare,* making what was to have been her last trip of the season, had to pull into a slough off the Tanana River because of dropping water and a hard freeze. The crew walked to Chena, a trip that took nearly two weeks, then rode the railroad the rest of the way to Fairbanks.

Chapter 9. Fairbanks Puts Down Roots

The years 1906 through 1909 saw Fairbanks peaking its early development; 1906 was the first year there was year-round mining. This made the town much more economically stable which, in turn, contributed to the permanence of the community. One factor that made year-round mining possible was the use of boilers. By 1907, the total capacity of boilers in use in the Tanana Valley exceeded 7,000 horsepower.[1] In 1906, $9,320,000 worth of gold was mined while in 1909 there was $9,650,000. After 1909, the bonanza placer mines began to play out and gold production by small operators was on the decline.

However, by the time gold production was no longer the central contributing factor to Fairbanks' development, many of the factors that led to the development of a permanent community already were established. Robert A. Monahan cites five typical major factors leading to the permanence of a settlement:

"1. Diversification of the economic base,
2. effective transportation and communication facilities,
3. organized social institutions,
4. an effective political system with enough power to operate and finance public utilities,
5. conveniences, comforts, aesthetic entertainment and other social pleasures...."[2]

Factors one, two and five all relied directly on steamboats during the first 20 years of Fairbanks' development. Steamboats played a vital part in diversifying Fairbanks' economy as the town developed into the central supply station of the

Interior, supplying communities up and down the Tanana River and on the Yukon. Steamboats were basically the only transportation available. Again, the short shipping season was a fatal weakness of steamboating and for this reason the boats eventually were replaced by the railroad. However, early on, all of the amenities came to the community by steamboat, from pianos to traveling acting groups. Fairbanks also kept abreast of the nation in communications. She had newspapers, telegraph service and, before 1908, the wireless had reached central Alaska. In the summer of 1908, wireless was installed on the river boats *Sarah* and *Isom*.[3]

In May 1906, just as one of the biggest mining years was about to begin, the business core of Fairbanks burned to the ground. The fire encompassed the area between Turner and Lacey streets and between First and Third avenues.[4] While the town's regular fire crew fought the fire from the shore, three steamboats tied up at the N.C. Co. dock. The *Tanana,* the *Seattle No. 3* and the *Schwatka* turned their fire hoses on the blaze.[5] Typical of the civic pride the people had in their town and in their ability to succeed, the mayor turned down offers of help from outside of the town with the statement, "We are still on the pay streak and need no assistance."[6] In addition to the sawmills that were already in existence, another one, the Independent Lumber Company, opened the next day and they all went into top production — with no rise in price — to supply the lumber needed for rebuilding. Every business was rebuilt, some starting construction the day after the fire, with the banks giving easy term loans, according to the May 23 issue of the *Fairbanks Daily Times.*

Other than the fire, the only setback to the growth of Fairbanks was from new "strikes." Whenever news of a new gold strike reached the town, there was a rush of men to the new site. If the strike continued to look good, more men would go. However, during this time the only strike that had any really significant effect was the one at Iditarod in 1910.[7]

Fairbanks Daily Times, August 25, 1908

ST. JOSEPH'S HOSPITAL IS MAKING IMPROVEMENTS

New Sidewalk is Being Built Under Supervision of Father Monroe.

The management of St. Joseph's hospital is making a decided improvement in the way of a new board walk which is being laid both in front and at the side of the hospital. Father Monroe is superintending the work, which is being done rapidly.

No new patients are reported and these already confined there are improving rapidly.

All the patients at St. Matthew's are getting along very nicely.

By 1906-07, about 5,000 people lived in the Fairbanks area. The town now had four churches, a school, three banks, and two hospitals.[8] Some 71,955 pounds of mail were received via steamboats in 1906, between May 22 and September 12. One shipment alone in September was five tons, including school supplies for the coming year.[9]

The 1907 summer mail contract between Tanana and Fairbanks via Chena called for at least six round trips per month, June through September, in "safe steamboats." Way points would be included and the pursers of the boats would act as the post office clerks, with no extra pay.[10]

During the winter of 1907-08, from October 1 to May 30, 60 overland mail trips between Fairbanks and Valdez were made each way. In all, 43,465 pounds came to Fairbanks and 22,575 pounds of mail went to Valdez.[11] Despite all the mail that was carried that winter, overland facilities were not sufficient to carry all the incoming mail to Fairbanks. The winter mails had weight limits and anything above those limits had to wait until spring and the return of the steamboats. In June of 1908 there were about eight tons of mail waiting in Whitehorse for the river to open.[12] This included some packages intended for Christmas 1907, a plum pudding for the past Thanksgiving and even some long underwear mailed the previous September.[13] Steamboats hauled the heavy mail throughout the summer. The July 9 *Fairbanks Daily News* reported that 44,200 pounds had come in on the last five boats. Launches were being used also, because they were faster and not as hampered by shallow water.[14] That winter, a new contract was drawn up for more mail to be carried including a "special mail" allowance of up to 24,000 pounds.[15]

As the Fairbanks-Valdez winter trail was improved, it began to be used for things other than mail and individual travel. In 1905 the Fairbanks-Valdez Stage Company (Ed. S. Orr & Co., Props.) was incorporated. According to the 1907 *Directory of the Tanana Valley* it employed 150 horses and 50 men. The cost for a passenger to go to Valdez was $125 and $150 for a passenger to come from Valdez to Fairbanks. A one-way trip took seven to 10 days. Some freight was carried, at a rate of 75 cents per pound for small quantities and 50 cents per pounds for large quantities.[16] During the winter of 1906-07 the stage made two weekly trips, carrying a total of 2,500 people [sic] and 2,000 tons of freight.[17] After construction work in 1909, there was talk that cars would be able to drive on the trail that winter.[18]

The cost of living in Fairbanks was high. Major reasons for this were the exorbitant cost of freight and the extraordinary expense of merchants who were able to receive merchandise for only a short period of time each year. Because merchants had to order enough in the summer to last for a year, they usually needed warehouses. Both stores and warehouse had to be heated all winter; there was the extra cost of storing and moving the merchandise; insuring the merchandise and the warehouse; and covering losses due to spoilage or from over-estimating the community's needs during the winter.[19] All these factors made for high prices, increasing as the winter progressed. A visitor to Fairbanks described the cost of living: "He that imagines that luxury does not exist in our far northern camps would need settle but one small bill for furnishing to become entirely convinced of the luxury of all things, even a sack of flour."[20]

Bunnell Collection, UAF archives

The *S.S. Susie* lands at the International Boundary (foreground, right), marking the border between Alaska and Canada, in about 1905.

Selid-Bassoc Collection, UAF archives

The *Flora* was typical of the smaller, shallow-draft boats used on the upper Tanana River and Chena Slough. Though plainer than her bigger sisters, the *Flora* played an important role in early-day transportation in Interior Alaska.

C. Waugaman Collection

The steamer *Tana* every year took Fairbanks school children on a picnic outing on the Tanana River, below Fairbanks. Local businessmen underwrote the cost.

C. Waugaman Collection

The *Tanana* is seen at the N.C. Docks at Fairbanks in about 1906. This handsome sternwheeler was one of the better-known vessels serving the city.

C. Waugaman Collection

The *S.S. Alaska* is seen amid "brash," or drift ice, probably on the Tanana River. The *Alaska* was a frequent visitor to Fairbanks.

C. Waugaman Collection

A fine example of a boat built specifically for the upper Tanana and Chena Slough trade, and other shallow streams, the *Tanana* was a handsome, fast and profitable vessel. She was one of the first to offer electric lights in passenger cabins.

C. Waugaman Collection

The *Tanana* came to an unhappy end, sinking in 1921. She had been considered one of the fastest shallow-draft boats on the rivers, once traveling from St. Michael to Fairbanks in five days, 17 hours of running time.

Ralph McKay Collection, UAF archives

Not all sternwheelers were things of grace and beauty, as evidence the *A.J. Goddard*, built on Lake Bennett and sailed down the Yukon to Dawson during the Klondike gold rush.

Selid-Bassoc Collection, UAF archives

The *May*, a chain-driven sternwheeler, was one of the more bizarre vessels seen on the Yukon River in 1898. This photograph carried a caption, "Dawson or Bust."

C. Waugaman Collection

The crew of the steamer *Reliance*, circa 1911.

C. Waugaman Collection

Chena, once thriving on the Tanana River just downriver from where the Chena flows into the Tanana, was an early rival of Fairbanks. The *Julia B*, a frequent visitor to Fairbanks, is one of the steamboats tied up at the bank.

Bunnell Collection, UAF archives

During its hey-day, Chena was a wintering-over place for several steamboats at the end of each season.

C. Waugaman Collection

Chena was well planned and platted, using the names of U.S. battleships for its street names. A picturesque town on the banks of the Tanana River, Chena ultimately was abandoned as Fairbanks became the Interior's dominant city politically and economically.

C. Waugaman Collection

Passengers, presumably miners, waited to go aboard the steamer *Rock Island* at Chena (also known as Chenoa) in about 1904.

MacKay Collection, UAF archives

Three regular visitors to Fairbanks during the height of the steamboat era were, from left, the *Delta*, the *Rock Island* and the *Tanana.*

Bunnell Collection, UAF archives

A wide-angle view of Fairbanks as seen from Garden Island across the Chena Slough on June 15, 1905.

Bunnell Collection, UAF archives

Samson Hardware can be seen through the trees in the middle of this panoramic photograph of Fairbanks taken in about 1906.

The *Fairbanks Evening News,* on September 26, 1906, stated that merchants made little money during the summer and now must raise their prices or face a loss. Prices started to climb in late September. In 1906, merchants predicted price increases in sugar, cream, butter, canned fruits (because they were short in supply), and potatoes. They went on to say that there would be no rise in price for flour, onions, tea, coffee, or spices. In 1908 price increases started by the first part of September, mainly, according to *The Fairbanks Daily News* of September 20, because there were 10,000 people in the area and goods were already short. Cream ran short by spring and always was in heavy demand. In 1909, the April 5 *The Fairbanks Daily News Miner* said that the community consumed 40 cases a day.

Fairbanks Sunday Times, September 6, 1908

NEW SKATES ARRIVE FOR THE ROLLER RINK

Steam Heat Will Be Turned on For the Public This Evening.

The new Richardson skates have arrived for the roller rink and will be ready for the public this evening. The rink will open at the usual hour. The hall is now connected with steam heat and will prove warm and comfortable.

With the approach of cold weather, the rink is becoming a more popular resort and shows an increased attendance each evening it is opened to the public.

Fairbanks continued to develop as a family town. By 1908, on the first day of school there were 111 primary students and 16 secondary students in the Fairbanks public school. There were also 13 students attending the new school on Garden Island across the river. Attendance picked up as the fall progressed and more children came in from the creeks.[21]

Fairbanks Evening News, August 20, 1906

SPECIAL 1/4 OFF SALE

1/4 Off all Silk Petticoats

1/4 Off all Walking Skirts

$^{1}/_{4}$ Off all Wash & Silk Waists
$^{1}/_{4}$ Off all Muslin Underwear
$^{1}/_{4}$ Off all Summer Hosiery
$^{1}/_{4}$ Off all Summer Kimonos
$^{1}/_{4}$ Off all Corsets

Merchants' advertisements in Fairbanks papers throughout 1906-1909 show the domestic interests of the community as well as the mining camp's needs: bedspreads, sheets and pillowcases, "cabin linings," tapestries, burlap, denim, couch covers, table covers, embroidery silks, notions, lace curtains, cloth coats and suits, fur coats, fur-lined coats, fur scarves, caps, mitts, cashmere hose, blankets, comforts, plain and figured silkaline, rosebushes, the "swellest line of skirts" (silks, voiles, panama, serge and mannish tweeds), golf coats, corsets, perfumes, combs and novelties, furniture, carpets, rugs, linoleum, crockery, pictures, moldings, rockers, tea and house gowns, fancy wrappers in newest shades, fur coats from St. Paul, wolf robes, and oysters.

Fairbanks Daily Times, August 25, 1903

LADIES' EVENING IS POSTPONED ONE WEEK

Arctic Brotherhood Will Join in the Recognition to Judge Wickersham.

Owing to the fact that the reception to Judge Wickersham will be held this evening, the ladies evening at the A.B. meeting has been postponed until a week from tonight.

Social organizations were popular in the young town, including a "Masonic Lodge, an aerie of Eagles, a camp of the Arctic Brotherhood, one theater, two public halls, the Tanana Club, a strong social organization composed of the representative businessmen and miners of the community, a curling club, and ladies clubs."[22]

And, just as Mr. Joe Field predicted in the August 13, 1906, *Fairbanks Evening News,* "This town will prove a central supply station or depot for the prospectors to draw upon ..." because of the opening and rapid development of mining in the area. In 1906 the Tenderfoot mining region was booming and independent steamboats, including the *White Seal* and the *Florence S.*, shipped 707 tons of freight upriver. At the end of the navigation season, an additional 500 tons could not be delivered to the new mining camp but it was "extra" (mostly machinery) and not essentials.[23]

By 1908, supplies including boilers were being sent to the mining areas along the Innoko and Koyukuk rivers. On May 26, 1909, the *Little Delta* set out pushing a barge with two horses, feed, and a portion of a mining outfit for the Koyukuk. The rest of the summer she would run on the upper river.[24] The small steamer *Pup* started May 25 with nine men and odds and ends of freight for the Kantishna.[25]

On May 25, the *Luella* hauled a few passengers and five tons of freight for the Innoko District. She planned to pick up more freight at Ft. Gibbon where she was to meet some other boats coming from the upper Yukon. Her main consignment was materials to replenish the stock in Billy Barrett's outfit.[26] And on May 22, the *Martha Clow* also was scheduled to leave for the Innoko district.[27]

Billy Munson decided in 1909 to build a warehouse to serve the Salchaket country on the upper Tanana apparently because miners were unhappy with freight being offloaded on the bank indiscriminately by the freighters.[28] Through this time period (1906-1909), the new mines, from the upper Tanana to the tributaries of the lower Yukon, relied on steamboats using Fairbanks as a central supply station, to haul supplies to their camps.

Fairbanks Daily Times, August 25, 1908

Tanana Valley Railroad
Time Table No. 1

Chena and Fairbanks

No. ___ Mixed Daily

8:00 a.m. 1:00 p.m. Leave . . . . Chena
8:25 a.m. 1:30 p.m. Leave . . . . Junction
8:45 a.m. 1:45 p.m. Arrive . . . . Fairbanks

Fairbanks and Chatanika

North Bound
No. 3 Mixed, Daily

Leave 1:15 p.m. . . . . Fairbanks
Leave 1:30 p.m. . . . . Junction
Leave 1:40 p.m. . . . . Easter
Leave 2:20 p.m. . . . . Eldorado
Leave 2:55 p.m. . . . . Fox
Meet 3:30 p.m. . . . . Gilmore
Leave 4:15 p.m. . . . . Ridgetop
Leave 4:50 p.m. . . . . Olnes
Leave 5:26 p.m. . . . . Chatanika

Between Fairbanks and Fox

North Bound

9:45 a.m. 3:30 p.m. Lv . . . . Fairbanks
9:55 a.m. 3:40 p.m. Lv . . . . Junction
10:00 a.m. 3:45 p.m. Lv . . . . Ester
10:25 a.m. 4:10 p.m. Lv . . . . Eldorado
10:45 a.m. 4:30 p.m. Lv . . . . Fox

Chena, although not booming, still was in business during these years. She still had, according to a Chena merchant, a large amount of business "from the steamer trade and miners continue to drop in from Ester Creek and the other creeks in back of Chena ... Even though rival fish camps are starting in Fairbanks, we feel no resentment, for we are doing all the business we can handle."[29] According to the 1907 *Directory,* Chena had an electric light plant, telephones, two docks, a log jail, a school house, a saw mill, a volunteer fire department, telegraph office, railroad repair shop and roundhouse, hospital and an amusement hall that seated 500. In 1908, some new buildings and a new road to Ester were under construction, but a Fairbanks newspaper somewhat patronizingly called it "a busy little town these days" during the height of the freighting season.[30] Another article that fall, however, described Chena as the "biggest seaport in the Interior ... with an extensive railroad terminal, a complete system of docks and warehouses...."[31]

Chapter 10. Boat Building

As long as the waterways and steamboats were important in Fairbanks' continuing growth, waterfront activity in the town continued to develop. In 1905, just four years after Barnette's disgruntled arrival on the riverbank, the *White Seal,* a 194-ton steamboat, was built in Fairbanks. In 1910, the 272-ton *Samson* was built. Small craft such as poling boats and "other river craft" also were built along the waterfront.

By the summer of 1909, the river banks echoed: Hammers whacked, saws rasped, laborers and carpenters whistled and called, sawdust and chips swirled in the current. A Mr. McDonald built over 40 scows that season, ranging in size from 16 to 40 feet and selling for \$25 to \$175.[1] Indeed, several men were in the scow business that year. One of them built a scow for the *Martha Clow* "across the river near the hospital" using all native lumber. There was some thought for a plant for building boats of all sizes.[2]

Fairbanks Sunday Times, September 6, 1908

IS RESCUED FROM WATER A FOOT DEEP IN GASOLINE SIDE-WHEELER

Billy Greer, George Newcombe and Jack Cambridge sneaked back to town late Thursday night in the latter's gasoline side-wheeler, after an absence of several days in the Salchaket country on a hunting expedition.

Greer reports an excellent time — an outing replete with amusing incidents and an absence of game. On the up-trip both Rusk and Newcombe were swept overboard by hanging trees and narrowly escaped drowning. Rusk effected *his own and Newcombe's rescue by discovering in the nick of time that the water was only a foot deep.*

Numerous sidewheelers were built during the summer of 1909, mainly by men who then used them to travel to the new mining camps.[3] William Appleby and Ed Uhl wanted a steamboat that could go wherever a launch could go. They built a "trim little 20 horsepower sidewheeler steamer," especially for light-draft navigation and speed on the swift, shallow streams. The boiler was light-weight, but with a large heating surface. The hull was housed over with a substantial roof and canvas sides. It had the advantage of a launch yet was large enough for "quite a passenger list and considerable amount of freight."[4]

Three old-timers constructed the *Marathon,* another sidewheeler, in the Chena Slough. With five men and seven tons of supplies and mining equipment aboard, they set out for the Iditarod mining camp. There they dismantled the boat and used the machinery to set up a sawmill.[5] Another sidewheeler was wrecked 25 miles below Chena, losing its entire three-ton outfit.[6]

Shipbuilding wasn't the only waterfront activity. In 1906, the N.C. Co. announced plans to build a 60' x 100' x 25' warehouse the following year. The upper warehouse of the old Alaska Commercial Company in Dawson was to be torn down and shipped to Fairbanks on one of the first boats of the 1907 season and rebuilt here.[7] Some businessmen put in a new wharf just below the Arctic Shooting Gallery in 1906. Unfortunately, the *Lotta Talbot,* which burned when the Riverside Hotel caught fire, sank right at the landing of this new wharf.[8]

In 1909, N.A.T.&T., needing a loading dock and warehouse in Fairbanks, utilized the barge, *Erie.* The *Erie* was 172' x 38' with a 1,000-ton capacity and was moored near the Masonic Temple.[9] Healy and Parsons built two warehouses on the north side of the river opposite St. Matthew's Hospital.[10]

Chapter 11. Steamboats on the Chena

From 1906-1909 the two main freight companies, Northern Navigation Company and North American Transportation & Trading Company, as well as numerous independent firms, fought for the lion's share of riverboat trade. The rivalry between the two big companies was grim, but they were united in their indignation with the small, independent lines.

As the 1906 shipping season began, the two large companies agreed that should any independent steamers get stuck on a sandbar and need to be pulled off, their steamboats would charge $100 an hour to help. On her first trip of the season, the independent *Monarch* got stuck, but because of her position on the sandbar, the big boats could offer no assistance. It took the *Monarch* three days to work herself off, but she never got stuck again that season. Late in the season the N.A.T.&T.'s *Power* ran onto a sandbar. Her crew tried all the tricks but could not free her. She was stranded for a week before another steamboat came along — the *Monarch*, as fate would have it. Twenty-four hours of winching and tugging ensued before the *Power* was free. The *Monarch* sent her on her way with good cheer — and a bill for $2,400.[1]

As the population of Fairbanks grew, the amount of freight shipped in also increased. The following tonnages appear in the 1907 *Directory of the Tanana Valley*:

1904 . . . . 12,000 tons
1905 . . . . 20,000 tons

1906 . . . . 23,000 tons
1907 . . . . 36,000 tons (estimated)[2]

Despite the increase in freight, shipping rates remained high. In 1904, while freight only cost $15-$35 per ton from Seattle to Nome or St. Michael, it cost $135-$220 per ton between Seattle and Fairbanks via St. Michael. The freight companies blamed the high cost of operating riverboats, the short season for navigation, the many navigation hazards along the northern rivers, and fluctuation of river travel.[3] Their detractors pointed accusingly at the virtual monopoly of the two large freight companies.[4] In 1908, it cost $800 to ship an automobile from Ohio to Fairbanks.[5]

In 1909, the Schubach and Hamilton Steamship Company considered trying to break the price monopoly but in the April 5 *Fairbanks Daily News Miner,* it was announced that it had reached an agreement with N.A.T.&T., and there would be no price war that year.

The Alaska Steamship Company in late May 1909 did cut its rates between Puget Sound and Nome/St. Michael. However, the cut did not apply to traffic up the Yukon River and its tributaries, so had little impact on Interior Alaska.[6] Freight rates remained high until steamboats declined as the major means of transportation. The same was true of passenger rates, except for brief reductions during price wars. Passenger rates from Fairbanks to the Outside were listed in the September 9, 1909, *Fairbanks Daily News Miner*:

via Dawson	$130 first class	$115second class
via St. Michael	$110 first class	$65 second class

Fairbanks Daily News Miner, June 6, 1908

AUTO COMING TO FAIRBANKS

SEATTLE, June 6 — The Stanley Dollar, of the Dollar line of steamers, sailed for Nome this afternoon, carrying a large cargo of freight and a capacity load of passengers, most of them for the Tanana and other interior points.

In the cargo was an automobile for Fairbanks and two for Nome. Both of them are splendid machines, and built to withstand the rough usage of the Northern trails.

As Fairbanks diversified, so did the freight unloaded from the boats. Smith's Gun Shop received Bicycle playing cards[7] and Pacific Cold Storage announced the arrival of its refrigerator steamer, the *Robert Kerr,* with a full supply of meats including poultry and oysters.[8] Four Keystone drills, each weighing several tons, arrived in the fall[9] along with some cast steel-top camp stoves, number seven or eight Steel ranges and a full line of Air Tight heaters.[10] Six stage coaches for the Fairbanks-Valdez winter trail came in on the *Koyukuk*[11] and new railroad cars including a locomotive and rails, all for the Tanana Mines Railroad, rumbled off the steamboat in the fall of 1906.[12] What may have been the first automobile for the Interior arrived in June, 1908.[13] Autos were popular in the Interior and by 1911, with nine cars on the streets, Fairbanks had more autos than any other Alaskan city.[14] The July 24, 1908, *Fairbanks Daily News* announced that the *Tanana* had delivered the first watermelon of the year (in addition to other perishable goods, 91 sacks of mail and 122 passengers). And in July, the missing part of the hose wagon came on the *St. Michael.*[15] A small newspaper plant, previously used in Chena by the *Tanana Miner,* was shipped in the spring of 1908 to the Innoko District. The venture failed, and it made a return trip in the fall.[16] In September 1908 the N.C. Co. dock held 17 boilers, the smallest of which was 40 horsepower.[17]

Livestock were herded off the steamboats in increasing numbers. Over a period of five days (September 20-25, 1906) the *Fairbanks Evening News* reports that 140 pigs and 12 calves came to Fairbanks from Chena by train, direct off a steamboat at Chena. Approximately 300 sheep were driven to a pasture three miles from town. The pigs were kept at the slaughterhouse yards until the first good cold snap. (At that time, 20 beef cattle a day were being butchered in preparation for winter.) And the largest livestock shipment yet was expected to bring 199 cattle and 25 calves, which also would go out to pasture. Another 50 young cattle arrived on the next steamer and were driven to a pasture eight miles from town. There were about 80 cows in various meadows around town.

The fall of 1908 was the first time local businesses tried shipping in livestock via St. Michael instead of Dawson.[18] Several hundred cattle came in that year, in addition to hogs and sheep.[19] In July 1909, 3,750 live laying hens and broilers cackled their way to Fairbanks aboard the *Hamilton* and *Schwatka.* Laying hens sold for $2.50 to $3.00 each and the broilers for 50 cents a pound.[20] The shipment of live beef increased more than five times from the previous year. Pacific Cold Storage shipped in some 1,100 cattle and 550 sheep, with another 650 sheep herded over the trail from Valdez. Waechter and Gardner shipped 1,000 cattle and 250 sheep (650 overland from Valdez) and some calves and hogs.[21]

The early freight of the season tended to be perishables and general merchandise. Grain, hay, and heavy goods came next, then machinery with orders for just about everything in a mad dash at the end, but with food always a top priority.[22]

The N.C. Co. built a "billboard" in front of its transportation office to post the comings and goings of the steamboats, which were of vital interest to everyone. The board displayed a chart with boat models that moved about to show the locations of the various boats. The newspapers issued daily steamer bulletins when possible, giving the location and/or problems of any of the boats on any of the rivers.

Trying to guess when the river would close down for the season and trying to land all freight at its proper destination created plenty of worry for the shipping companies. In 1906, the navigation season wrap-up news began with *The Fairbanks Evening News* reporting on September 24 that the N.C. Co. still had 1,250 tons of freight to bring in, but that the company was confident it could do it. Of that total, 750 tons were at Ft. Gibbon with the *Koyukuk, Delta* and *Tanana* to bring it in. The company looked for the last 500 tons from Dawson on the *Ida May* the next day. The N.A.T.& T. had 1,700 tons to come, 500 of which were on the Tanana River. The remaining 1,200 tons would be brought by the *Ella, Weare,* and *Healy,* with the option of leasing the *Crimmins* and perhaps the *White Seal* if necessary. By October 1, the N.A.T.& T. had 1,100 tons either at Ft.

Gibbon or on the Tanana River. The N.C. Co. still had four boats running on the Tanana: the *Tanana, Margaret, Koyukuk,* and *Isabelle.*

As of October 2, ways had been built close to town for boats running on the Tanana River. By October 16, the N.C. Co. boats *Tanana, Margaret* and *Delta* were at Fairbanks for the winter and the *Isabelle* was at Chena. N.A.T.& T. boats wintered at Dawson and St. Michael. N.A.T.& T. reported that it had hauled 10,000 tons of freight to Fairbanks that season, almost twice what it had hauled the year before.

The 1908 season got off to a slow start, only one boat with merchandise from Outside reaching Fairbanks by June 22.[23] Three months later, on September 25, *The Fairbanks Daily News* noted gloomily that the outlook was not promising, with 3,500 tons of winter supplies not yet delivered to Fairbanks and Chena, and fresh ice in the Chena that morning. However, on September 28, the Tanana River had risen five inches in the previous 24 hours and by the next day the entire 3,500 tons were at Ft. Gibbon or aboard steamboats running up the Tanana River. By October 1, some bad spots in the river had been washed clear and the river was still high, but nobody was letting their boilers cool down. N.A.T.& T. dispatched the *Tanana* and *Barr* to Gibbon for the last 250 tons. The *Healy* had left Gibbon the day before with 375 tons (90 of which were for Manley Hot Springs). The *Nunivak,* with 500 tons, dropped part of her cargo at the Hot Springs, and the *Monarch* was on her way down to help her. By October 8, it was announced there might still be 25 to 50 tons in Dawson. There were 1,000 tons on the Tanana River but all was within 50 miles of Chena. Hay and grain had been cached at different places on the shore between Fairbanks and the Hot Springs when low water forced the captains to lighten their boats. However, a last-minute reprieve prolonged the season a few more days. The October 11 *Fairbanks Daily News* reported that every last pound of N.A.T.& T.'s freight was in and that the *Monarch* would arrive in Chena that day. Merchants were so swamped with incoming freight during this final rush that at least one of them closed early so the clerks could get all of the merchandise out.[24] The steamboat company officials were "much elated over the fact that all predictions as to a food shortage this winter had been knocked in the head."

That winter the *Weare, Barr* and *Evelyn* were laid up in the Salchaket Slough. The *Hamilton* and *Healy* made full speed to Dawson before freeze-up.[25]

Even though all the freight got in, there were shortages in such basic items as butter, potatoes, sugar and beef by spring of1909. The shortages were severe enough that some stores had to close.[26] Thus, when the Tanana River opened in the spring, no time was wasted trying to get these "shorts" into Fairbanks. The steamer *Tanana* made a run down to the Hot Springs and returned on May 19 with 22 tons of native potatoes and one ton of sugar. On the 20th she left again, this time for Ft. Gibbon with 35,000 feet of lumber from the Tanana Mill Company, a million dollars in gold, 30 passengers and three tons of mail. From Ft. Gibbon she headed up the Yukon until she met the *Susie* coming from Dawson. Relieving the *Susie* of a few passengers and 118 head of cattle, she wheeled about and steamed for Fairbanks again where she paused to pick up an additional 38 hogs on her way past the Hot Springs.[27] The *White Seal* left Whitehorse with three barges and whistled into Chena and Fairbanks May 31 with eggs, onions, lemons, bacon, cheese, sugar, tobacco and other shortages.[28] The *Tana* arrived on June 3 from Dawson with more perishables and shortages.[29] The big 718-ton *D.H. Campbell* also put out from Dawson with freight to relieve the Fairbanks situation. She made Chena on May 26 and lightened some of her load so she could get up the low Chena Slough to Fairbanks. With her delivery of liquor, canned goods, cream, sugar, butter and beef, prices began to drop back to normal for these shorts.[30]

Life on the river was hard work and long hours but it was not all drudgery. That summer of 1909, presumably when the water levels were up, the *Tanana, Koyukuk* and the *Schwatka* raced from Tanana to Fairbanks. The three boats passed and repassed each other again and again. Passengers helped with loading when they made firewood stops for the greedy furnaces. On one of the *Koyukuk's* stops, they loaded eight cords in 11 minutes! The *Schwatka* and the *Tanana* had the greater power, but they also had the heaviest loads. *Tanana* came in first at Chena, *Koyukuk* second and *Schwatka* third. The first two places were reversed by the time they reached Fairbanks and a festive mood prevailed as the three boats unloaded their 200 passengers and 600 tons of freight.[31]

By September 15, the river was low again and the big boats were struggling over the Tanana sandbars as far as they could while more shallow-draft steamers lightered to Chena and Fairbanks. By October 4, all the freight was above Nenana and there were just 500 tons out. But there was no last-minute reprieve this year. The boats were caught between Twelve Mile Slough and the Tolovana River with their 500 tons of freight, mostly feed and a large boiler.[32]

The unpredictability of freeze-up or low water not only caused freight to be stranded sometimes, it occasionally stranded steamboat crews as well. In 1960, "Steamboat Bill" Heckman recalled working on the *Portus B. Weare* in the fall of 1906. It was supposed to be the last trip of the season up the Tanana River, but the boat couldn't get into the mouth of the Tanana. The water was too low and ice was starting to form, so the crew put the boat into a nearby slough. Most of the men took off walking to Chena, a trip that took them 13 1/2 days. There Heckman took the train to Fairbanks in hopes of getting a ride out on one of the sleighs going to Valdez. However, all the sleighs were booked solid for the next several weeks. The N.A.T.& T. agent then offered him the price of his fare and roadhouse expenses if he had to walk to Valdez. So that is what Heckman did. It took him 16 days to walk 350 miles to Valdez. From there he took passage Outside for the winter. Undaunted by the misadventurous end to that riverboat season, he headed north the following spring again for another summer of steamboating.[33]

PART III:
Early Fairbanks' Declining Years (1910-1923)

Chapter 12. Survival by Diversity

Fairbanks Daily News Miner, August 6, 1921

THOSE OF RIGHT FAITH

With permission being talked by the thotless here, the thotful seem to be going ahead as tho nothing had or could happen which is not good. They are completing the flouring mill to be ready for the Fall-grinding of the wheat crop, and earnest citizens of financial standing who have nothing else to do are working as day laborers on the mill without pay, for the success of the enterprise and the good of the camp. They are building the living quarters at the Agricultural College & Bureau of Mines, and they are building well and swiftly.

The years 1910 to 1923 mark a decline in Fairbanks. Mining jobs ended as the small-time miners sluiced the last of the profitable gold. The population shrank as men drifted out of the failing mines and marched away to World War I. The steamboat traffic dwindled, too.

In 1909, gold production in the Fairbanks region hit an all-time high of $9,650,000. The next year it dropped to $6,242,000 and slipped steadily until 1920 when only $600,000 washed out of the muck. (See chart p. 91) The 4,682 people within a 25 mile radius of Fairbanks in 1910 declined to only 1,356 people 10 years later.[1] Stampedes to other mining districts accounted for some of this drop, but World War I drew away 75% of Fairbanks District's population.[2]

Fairbanks Daily News Miner, July 8, 1916

BOARD TELLS OF SCHOOL TABLETS

Announcement is made by the school board for the

benefit of the merchants that about 5,000 writing tables, 8 x 10 inches will be used during the coming year by the students of the public schools.

During the years when gold was king, mining seemed to be all that mattered in Fairbanks' growth and development. However, from the beginning many citizens believed Fairbanks was permanent and not just a gold rush town. The decline in gold production after 1909 was the real test of Fairbanks' ability to survive. Although the population was dwindling and businesses were hurting in 1916, Fairbanks still had five major churches, 200 students attending public schools, two daily newspapers and 45 miles of railroad to the mines.[3] The next year saw the permanent steel bridge across the Chena Slough at Cushman Street completed.[4] By 1919, the Territory was erecting the first modest hall of the Alaska Agriculture College and School of Mines a few miles out of town.[5] And in 1921 Garden Island was incorporated into Fairbanks.[6]

River transportation of the mail became more and more unsatisfactory. In 1911, mail came over the trails from Valdez 17 times in the 50 day period from March 3 to April 22. However, that summer during another 50 day period, June 20 through August 9, the mail arrived only seven times by boat.[7] By October 4, summer mail by river had arrived only 13 times and once 21 days had elapsed between deliveries.[8] (These statistics only represent the gaps between arrivals of mail-carrying steamboats, not necessarily all steamboat arrivals.)

The Fairbanks public wanted better mail service. They asked officials to improve the trail between Valdez and Fairbanks but the overland winter mail contract did not pay enough to permit hauling as many pounds of mail as was posted to Fairbanks. The heavy parcel post and second-class mail stacked up over the winter until the steamboats moved out the backlog in the summer. By late winter newspapers and magazines were scarce.[9] In 1914, the N.C. Co. decided to haul winter mail at least part way by automobile.[10] But it appears to have been 1917 before any summer mail rolled over the trail route.[11]

The post office felt the effects of population decline. In 1915 it was reduced to a third-class post office when transactions fell just $100 below the level required for second-class standing. Resourcefully, the local postal officials called for the populace to send stamps instead of money orders when mail-ordering goods from Outside.[12]

With the Fairbanks-Valdez trail established, people soon realized it was good for more uses than just winter transport of passengers and mail. In the fall of 1910, merchants talked of bringing in eggs over it. They had ordered enough for the winter but then filled so many orders to the Iditarod Camp that Fairbanks was running short.[13]

Four years later, the March 22, 1914, *Fairbanks Daily Times* reported "practically all merchants ... have large consignments coming either by stage or special rigs." They received eggs, fresh fruit, and shoes with the result that prices of staples remained steady all winter. By the end of March the last shipments that could be made over the trail before breakup were arriving.

In August 1911 the secretary of the interior visited Chitina, a mining town on the Copper River. An editorial in the August 26 *Fairbanks Daily Times* called on the secretary for assistance in improving the trail from Chitina to Fairbanks so that it could be traveled in two days. The improved trail connection to the Valdez port would allow travel to the Outside in eight days. Without trail improvements the most reliable route was the river system, requiring three to four weeks to reach Seattle. Moreover, the editor pointed out, the upgraded trail would challenge the monopoly of the steamboat companies, which had raised their rates 20 to 30 percent that year.[14]

In July 1914, Bob Sheldon drove the 325 miles from Chitina to Fairbanks in 34 hours running time (58$^1/_2$ hours actual time). The mud and the creek crossings were "adverse" but he averaged 10 miles per hour and his four passengers were pleased. Three cases of gasoline were required for the trip. He hoped to do it regularly and to make a round trip in 10 days.[15] A few days later, however, rains made the trail impassable.[16] According to the *Alaskan Engineering Commission Report* covering the period from

March 12, 1914, to December 31, 1915, summer auto passenger service had just started on the trail. By this time winter passenger service on the trail was considered excellent, and it carried about 100 tons of "emergency freight" each winter.[17] A 1916 booklet put out by the Chamber of Commerce of Fairbanks described the 310-mile road to Valdez as an excellent winter road, but expensive. With favorable conditions, the booklet claimed, cars could use it in the summer.[18]

The town of Chena suffered its death throes with the decline of the steamboat traffic. By 1911, *The Fairbanks Daily Times* was calling the town of Chena "a little village."[19] By 1916, buildings were being dismantled and hauled downriver to the former Indian village of Nenana,[20] located at the mouth of the Nenana River on the Tanana River about 65 miles below Chena, which had become the headquarters for the building of the Alaska Railroad in the Interior. Although longshoremen still populated Chena in the summer to handle the freight, the town was near its end. By 1916 the terminal yard of the Tanana Valley Railroad had been moved to Garden Island.[21] The last recorded merchandise landings at Chena were in 1917.[22] Hudson Stuck described Chena's demise as the "classic Alaskan instance of short-sighted greed that overreached itself and 'lost out'."[23]

Fairbanks, too, suffered as one business after another failed. During the gold mining boom, logging was an important support industry. When mining lost its glitter there was less need of lumber for such things as sluice boxes and buildings. In any case, trees were becoming scarce. In 1903, the first year of commercial logging, ample forests stood a short distance from town. By 1913, the trees had been cut a mile back from each side of the Chena River for 100 miles upstream,[24] and some of the sawmills were sent to new mining towns.[25]

But Fairbanks diversified and survived. It became a distribution center for the new mining camps that continued to appear. In 1913, a gold strike at Chisana sent stampeders high-tailing far up the Tanana River, where the Chisana and Nabesna rivers join to make the Tanana River. For more practical purposes Chena was the head of navigation on the Tanana, but small steamers always had forged up the Tanana River to the new sites. Hudson Stuck said that he saw or knew of six wrecks on the upper Tanana in the spring of 1917 when he traveled in the vicinity: the *Koyukuk*, the *Dusty Diamond*, the *S. & S.*, the *Atlas*, the *Tetlin*, and the *Samson*.[26] No new gold camps appeared in 1916, but a local merchant declared that they had sent more freight out of Fairbanks on steamboats to existing camps and towns than ever before. The outgoing freight had included farming tools and machinery.[27]

Fairbanks Daily News Miner, May 19, 1920

OUR FARMERS ARE PLOWING

> *According to information received from a recent visitor to the farms in the vicinity of Fairbanks, work along agricultural lines is about to commence in earnest. The soil formerly under cultivation, is drying out rapidly, and will soon be in shape to be prepared for the Spring sowing.*
>
> *The government farm began plowing yesterday, but horses are being used as the ground is not yet sufficiently dried out to bear the tractor.*
>
> *It is expected that all the farmers will be ploughing by the end of the present week and that an acreage far greater than in former years will be under cultivation this season.*

Farming in the Tanana Valley increased during these lean years. By 1914, many homesteads in the area produced surpluses of potatoes, carrots, cabbage and turnips for sale to other communities along the river including Iditarod and Ruby. In 1920 there were a record 1,700 acres reported under cultivation. This was due in part to the extra markets which included not only the mining camps, but also the new railroad camps. Railroad crews and the horses they used in the railroad construction consumed large quantities of food, which the farmers in the Tanana Valley were able to help provide. By 1920, grain production had increased to the point that the Fairbanks businessmen helped finance a flour mill.[28]

If the recoverable gold was gone, the romance of gold country remained. The miners wanted pay dirt, not romance, but a new kind of adventurer came in search of sights and sensations. Tourism began. The White Pass and Yukon Company operated special boats bringing groups of tourists down the Yukon and up the Tanana to Fairbanks where they could spend up to two days.[29] Townspeople did their best to show the tourists a good time and when the White Pass and Yukon discontinued this service in 1921, citing irregular schedules, Fairbanks was quick to contact other travel agents Outside to arrange tour trips for the next summer.[30] With the railroad coming through and the Fairbanks-Valdez road much more comfortable and reliable for summer travel, tourism showed real promise.

By 1918, Fairbanks was the Interior Alaska "shopping center." In September of that year the *Tanana* made a special trip to Nenana to bring people to Fairbanks for the "last shopping trip of the year" before the river froze over.[31]

Chapter 13. The Arrival of the Alaska Railroad

Visionary men of early Fairbanks knew that Interior Alaska could not keep growing unless it solved the problem of year-round, reliable transportation. Seasonal food shortages, the high cost of living, the depletion of available fuel in the area, and uncertain passenger and freight schedules all boiled down to one problem: The existing transportation systems were outmoded. In 1914-1915 a cord of wood in Fairbanks cost $11.25. It was estimated that one ton of coal, equivalent to two cords of wood, would cost five dollars delivered from the Nenana coal fields to Fairbanks by railroad (if only a railroad had existed). One quartz mill operator said this could save him $40 per day.[1]

Fairbanks Daily News Miner, June 6, 1921

RAILWAY TIME TABLE
Northern Division Alaskan Engineering Commission

Chatanika Sub-Division

Trains leave Fairbanks for Chatanika at 9:00 a.m. on Monday and Thursday; returning, leaves Chatanika at 1:10 p.m. of same days and arrive in Fairbanks at 4:20 p.m.

Fairbanks Sub-Division

Trains leave Fairbanks for Nenana at 8:00 a.m. on Tuesday and Friday; returning, leave Nenana 1:30 p.m. on same days and arrive in Fairbanks at 5:30 p.m.

Southbound arrives at Dunbar's station at 10:32 a.m. Northbound leaves Dunbar station at 3:38 p.m.

In 1915 the U.S. government decided to start construction on the railroad the following year. The tracks would reach from Seward to Fairbanks. Construction would take place from both ends, with a special effort for the leg between Fairbanks and Nenana.[2] In the summer of 1917, the U.S. government agreed to buy for approximately $300,000 the Tanana Valley Railroad which it had operated as a lease since 1916. In November 1919 the link between Fairbanks and Nenana was completed as a narrow gauge line.[3] (This narrow gauge railroad actually ended on the north side of the river at Nenana; the town proper was across the river.) From this important date, steamboat freight regularly became railroad freight at Nenana, ending the problem of shallow water on the Tanana River above Nenana and especially on the Chena River. In the same year Tanana Valley Railroad tracks were torn up,[4] but some boats still visited Fairbanks on occasion. *The Fairbanks Daily News-Miner* reported on August 2, 1921, that with "the exception of the *Tanana,* steamboats had been scarce articles here this year," and the *Tanana* had at that time only sailed from Fairbanks three times.

Not until May or early June 1923 was work finished on the railroad bridge connecting Nenana to the north side of the river and converting the tracks between Fairbanks and Nenana from narrow to standard gauge.[5] President Harding drove the golden spike that July, opening the new transportation system that saved 2,395 miles over the previous all-water route.[6]

Freight rates showed a marked improvement immediately. In 1923, the joint rates of water and rail were as follows (for a carload of freight):

groceries, mixed	$41 per ton
flour in sacks	$28 per ton
mining machinery (4,000 pounds)	$30 per ton
lumber, common, per 1,000 feet	$21.10 per ton[7]

A year earlier, the Alaska Railroad had established its River Boat Service, buying the *General Jacob* and *General Davis* from the U.S. Army. Probably in 1923, the Alaska

Railroad came to a gentleman's agreement with the Alaska-Yukon Navigation Company. The A.-Y.N. Co. would cover the upper Yukon River points, invading the Tanana only to pick up freight at Nenana. The A.R.R. Boat Service would cover the Tanana River and the lower Yukon.[8]

Chapter 14. The Fading of the Steamboats

Fairbanks Daily News Miner, August 6, 1919

AWFUL BLANK IN THE RIVER

Not Enough Activity in Steamboating to Maintain Common Interest

The steamboat bulletin today reads unlike the bulletins we used to have when steamboating was steamboating. Just take a look at it:

Selkirk — *Scheduled to leave Dawson for Eagle 8 p.m. 4th*
Dawson — *In Whitehorse, leaves on Friday.*
Casca — *up Carmacks, 8:30 p.m. the 4th*
Nasatlin — *In Whitehorse*
Alaska — *Down Nenana 3:45 a.m.*
Reliance — *Up McCarty 5 p.m., 5th for Tanana Crossing*
Lansing — *Left St. Michael for the States 5th*
Kotlik — *Down Marshall 2 a.m. 5th*
Julia B — *Up Birches 5:30 p.m., the 5th*
Davis — *At St. Michael*
Washburn — *Up Holy Cross for Dikeman, 4th*
Tanana — *At Fairbanks*
Sibilla. Kelly and Jacobs — *In Gibbon.*
Seattle 3 — *Up Kotlik midnight, 4th*
Yukon — *Up Circle 3 a.m., 3rd, the last report.*

Early in the period, 1910-1923, the Fairbanks waterfront bustled. A. Valentine built a small steamboat in 1910 in the yard of the Tanana Mill Company's old mill. Fifty-six feet long and 14 feet wide, she was square-nosed and intended exclusively for freight.[1] That same year a scow was built for the *Little Snug* on the north side of the slough.[2] In 1911 F.G. Noyes built two barges, each 24 feet by 90 feet, to be used to ship 250,000 feet of lumber with the *Julia B.* to the Iditarod River.[3] The *Idler*, 61 tons of steamboat, was also built in 1911.[4]

Sidewheelers still were being used and built in the early years of this period. The September 13, 1913, *Fairbanks Daily Times* notes that the little sidewheeler *Marie F.* left for the headwaters of the Tanana with several outfits and a couple of passengers. Her owner was Captain Finger. Earlier that summer another sidewheeler, the *Silver King,* was built to go to the Koyukuk River. Intriguing mention is made of a "gasoline auxiliary with power in the rear." The little craft was capable of carrying eight passengers and pushed a scow. The scow was fitted with bunks, a storage area for wood, gasoline, powder, machinery and other supplies for a full year. Owners expected the sidewheeler to be uniquely adaptable to the swift, shallow waters of the Koyukuk River and its tributaries. The sidewheel arrangement was supposed to be able to maneuver the boat where a rudder would be impractical.[5]

By 1915 the newspapers frequently mentioned launches, e.g., the *Dan*, the *Doman* and the *Midnight Sun*.[6] These small boats could carry a fair amount of freight and were used often on the shallow tributaries of the Tanana. The government used launches to transport people and freight between Nenana and Fairbanks during the construction of the railroad. The term "launch" was used rather loosely, but normally referred to smaller, shallow-draft boats driven by gasoline engines and with a single propeller at the rear. However, it is probable there were some steam launches, and perhaps even a few small stern-wheeled launches. Beyond this, we are unable to define more precisely what constituted a "launch" on an Interior river.

Freight companies also changed with the times. The Yukon Navigation Company in 1913 formed a subsidiary, the American-Yukon Navigation Company, to compete with the traffic which was supplying the Interior of Alaska from St. Michael. It built the *Yukon* and the *Alaska* especially for this purpose. The *Alaska* was 165 feet long with a beam of 35 feet and registered at 642 tons.[7] Her sister ship the *Yukon* was 211 feet long and 30 feet wide with "648 gross tons" carved on her hold beam. She had a passenger capacity of 98.[8] Both boats were designed especially to travel heavy downstream and light upstream. That was their job on the Yukon River, carrying freight from Dawson or Whitehorse to Fairbanks.[9]

In 1913, Alaska-Yukon Navigation Company and Northern Navigation Company, the last big freight shippers serving the Interior, became engaged in a rate war. It proved disastrous to both. In April 1914 the Alaska-Yukon Navigation Company bought out the Northern Navigation Company, including 96 steamers and barges.[10] This left the A.-Y.N. Co. as the only large shipper on the rivers, with an immense fleet of vessels — just in time for the decline in steamboating. In 1914 prices went back up, but not as high as they had been before the price war. Sample prices were:

Via St. Michael:
(with an additional $5.00 per ton after August 16)
hay, feed and blacksmith coal ..... $50 per ton
sugar, flour, cream (20,000 lb.) .... $52.50 per ton

Via Skagway:
(with 10% increase after September 10)
Class A (car lots) .... $59 per ton
Class B (car lots) .... $68 per ton
Class C (car lots) .... $83 per ton[11]

By mid-summer in 1914 there was no longer much freight going by way of St. Michael. Some shippers notified customers that their sailings to St. Michael would be indefinite and might even be cancelled.[12] At the same time it became easier to ship freight from Canada; Fairbanks was no longer an open port so it was no longer necessary to transfer the freight in Dawson.[13] Nevertheless freight rates still burdened the Interior economy. An automobile selling at $900 F.O.B. Detroit cost an additional $870.75 freight to Fairbanks. Farmers wanting to sell their produce to communities on the rivers were quoted high rates by A.-Y.N. Co. To send a ton of Fairbanks produce to Ruby, just a hundred miles down the Yukon from Ft. Gibbon, cost a farmer $30 —

although freight from Seattle to Ruby was only charged $40 per ton. To send produce to Dickman was even worse — the price was more than if it had come from Seattle. A miner's Keystone drill cost $808.75 for freight just from St. Michael to Ruby.[14] And rates for the upper Yukon River went up $6-$8 per ton in 1915.[15]

Costs for hauling supplies and equipment up some of the Tanana tributaries to mining camps sometimes reflected the unusual conditions. The Tolovana Transportation Company, a small independent company working out of Fairbanks, had a special set of rates for hauling supplies to Brooks, up the Tolovana River. They charged 1 1/2 cents per pound from Fairbanks to the Log Jam; 1/4 cent per pound for carrying it across the Log Jam; 1 1/2 cents per pound from the Log Jam to the West Port; and another 2 cents per pound from the West Port to Brooks.[16]

Another kink in the transportation system developed when Britain went to war with Germany and Austria. Canada then made a policy not to allow Germans and Austrians *out* of Canada. If people of either nationality were trying to leave Alaska to go to the United States, they had to go via St. Michael. If they were to go via Dawson, then they would be in Canada and not be allowed to leave — unless they were also citizens of the United States.[17]

Fairbanks Daily News Miner, July 7, 1922

MAKES TRIP ON YUKON IN LAUNCH

E.L. March, a tourist from Philadelphia, arrived in Fairbanks last evening, making the trip by way of White Horse and the Yukon.

Mr. March states that it is hard to get traveling accommodations on the Yukon from Dawson up, and that there were quite a number in Dawson waiting for the Alaska to bring them into the interior.

No one seemed to have any information as to when the Alaska would arrive, or where it was, so Mr. March together with a few others made the trip from Dawson to Tanana in gas launches and mail boats.

In 1922 when it was apparent that the railroad would be completed the following year, and that this would reduce steamboat freight into the Interior, A.-Y.N. Co. retaliated by withdrawing all service from the Tanana River and giving only intermittent service on the Yukon River with the *Alaska* and the *Yukon*. Small boats tried to relieve the situation by carrying freight to the Tanana River communities and to Fairbanks, but there were not enough. They even brought in the *General Jacob* to pick up stranded miners and trappers along the rivers.[18]

Steamboat freight deliveries between 1910 and 1923 reveal the life and changing enterprises of the community. In the August 22, 1912, *Fairbanks Daily Times* an advertisement announced that the following items had just arrived: buckboards, top buggies, road and heavy wagons, ploughs, harrows, and self-dumping rakes. An article on May 31, 1913, in the same newspaper indicated that rancher P.J. Rickert had ordered a thresher the previous winter and that another rancher, R.E. Cooley, had recently ordered a harvester and a binder—the first one for the Tanana Valley. On July 16, 1921, Vining ran an ad in the *Fairbanks Daily News Miner* that they had milk goats (for the first time) coming in on the *Tanana*. They would have both Toggenburgs and Saanens.

Farmers and meatpackers continued to bring in cattle, sheep, hogs and chickens both by trail from Chitina and by riverboat. With the slower-paced Fairbanks economy, less freight came in than during the boom era and it was not as newsworthy as previously. However, everyone still watched the paper for the arrival of new movies for Fairbanks' two movie theaters.[19]

Severe meat shortages plagued Fairbanks in the spring of 1913 and 1917. By May 7, 1913, the poultry and mutton were long gone, and only two weeks' supply of beef and pork remained despite the fact that some beef had been brought in over the trail. No new shipments were expected until around June 10.[20] Fairbanks was totally out of meat in May 1917. Merchants always planned their orders, expecting some hunting of meat to augment the supply, but game had been scarce that winter. To compound the problem, they had been unable to bring many live animals over the trail since there also was a shortage of feed.[21]

Viewed retrospectively, greed, poor planning, and perhaps a degree of stubbornness helped speed the demise of the grand ladies of the Interior rivers.

Gold in all its romance and complexity brought the Interior Alaska steamboat era to the high water of its glory. Twenty-three years later, the railroad ended river shipping. Fairbanks owed much of her beginning and her own early survival to steamboats, but at last, the steamboats met their demise because Fairbanks was finished with them.

Some Concluding Thoughts

When President Harding drove the Golden Spike signaling the birth of the Alaska Railroad, he also drove a nail in the coffin of steamboating to and from Fairbanks. As historian Terrence Cole, writing about the advent of the Alaska Railroad, put it: "The floating giants [steamboats] began to die out like a race of dinosaurs."[1] Cole was right. The arrival of the railroad dramatically reduced the time and money required to bring supplies and people to Fairbanks and other towns and camps in the Interior, and almost instantaneously brought about the demise of river traffic as the major mode of transportation.

This is not to say no more steamboats were to be seen. Indeed, the last passenger and cargo-carrying sternwheeler was running on the Yukon until May 1957. Ironically, the last steamboat was the *S.S. Nenana* operated by the Alaska Railroad and she docked finally at Alaskaland, a pioneer historical park in Fairbanks.

Even after the *Nenana* was laid up, diesel-powered boats continued sporadic service to Fairbanks. As nearly as we can determine, the *Yutana* in 1953 was one of the last boats carrying cargo in and out of the city with any regularity. Captain Jim Binkley testified in 1965 that "he last observed a commercial freighting operation in the summer of 1963 at which time the operation was taking place 300 yards upriver from the University Avenue bridge."[2]

> *"... a strong brown god — sullen, untamed and intractable..."*
>
> T.S. Eliot *Four Quartets*

"Our trip began auspiciously, with a perfect day, as to breeze and sunshine, and our boat threw the miles behind her with satisfactory dispatch."

Mark Twain *Life on the Mississippi*

Today, there is still a reminder of steamboating to be found in the presence of the tour boats *Discovery, Discovery II* and, now, *Discovery III*, all owned and operated by the Binkley family of Fairbanks. The company, founded by Captain Charles Madison "Jim" Binkley, son and grandson of rivermen, and his wife, Mary, began with a modest operation involving the *Godspeed*, formerly the cabin cruiser used by Alaska's third Episcopal bishop in carrying out his ministry. The Binkleys very quickly added to their fleet by building the *Discovery,* a chain-driven diesel excursion boat. The *Discovery II* was formerly the towboat, *Yutana*, operated by the Yutana Barge Lines, located in Nenana. Binkley brought her to Fairbanks and remodeled her as a chain-driven, diesel-powered sternwheeler. His first season of commercial operation was 1950. The company quickly became a major tourist attraction, carrying visitors some 10 miles down the Chena and Tanana rivers and back.

Although the Binkleys' boats are powered with modern diesel engines and meet contemporary safety standards, their colorful sternwheels and decorative smokestacks pay tribute to memories of the wonderful era when steamboats ruled the Chena, making Fairbanks the hub of the Interior.

Steamboating in Alaska was as exciting, dramatic and romantic as anywhere in the world. And there can be no doubt that steamboats played a preeminent role in the siting, founding and development of Alaska's second largest city.

Epilogue

A recurring story claims that the *Lavelle Young's* pilot house (wheel house) is to be found at Alaskaland, the historical pioneer park in Fairbanks. We believe that this is not the case. The *Lavelle Young* was dismantled in 1920, having all of her superstructure and machinery removed. Her hull then was converted into a "scow" (a type of barge as the word was used in early Alaska river lore) and used to haul freight about the rivers of Interior Alaska. On the barge, which still bore the name *Lavelle Young*, there was a "dog house" or "wannigan," a sort of deck house for lines, supplies and, presumably, a crude shelter. It was on that deck house that the barge's name was painted. This, in turn, led to confusion for historians trying to track the whereabouts of the *Lavelle Young* and her final demise. When the wreck was identified in 1979 at McGrath and a structure removed to Alaskaland, it was assumed that it was the pilot house of the steamboat when, in reality, we are reasonably sure that it was the deck house. This will explain why the pieces of wood lying on the ground at Alaskaland — though bearing the name *Lavelle Young* — never could be made to look like the pilot house from the old workhorse steamboat. While this may disappoint a few people, we are happy to set at rest an on-going argument as to the origin of the structure.

Charts

Gold Production in the Fairbanks Area 1903–1923

Year	Dollar value of gold
1903	$ 40,000
1904	400,000
1905	6,000,000
1906	9,320,000
1907	7,845,000
1908	9,180,000
1909	9,650,000
1910	6,242,000
1911	4,608,000
1912	4,371,000
1913	3,677,000
1914	2,739,000
1915	2,638,000
1916	1,839,000
1917	1,358,000
1918	827,000
1919	772,000
1920	600,000
1921	608,000
1922	747,000
1923	628,000

Source: Robert L. Monahan, who extracted the data from U.S. Department of the Interior, *Mineral Industry of Alaska,* U.S. Geological Survey, various bulletins, 1902-1944.

Landings at Fairbanks or Chena by Name and Frequency*

1903

Isabelle (1)
John J. Healy (1)
Koyukuk (1)
Tanana Chief (1)

1904

Cudahy (1)
Florence S. (1)
Koyukuk (1)
Lavelle Young (1)
Rock Island #1 (1)
Tanana (1)

1905

Cudahy (3)
Delta (2)
D.R. Campbell (1)
Ella (2)
Florence S. (1)
John L. Healy (2)
Lavelle Young (1)
Luella (1)
Margaret (1)
Minneapolis (1)
Portus B. Weare (3)
Rock Island #1 (1)
Schwatka (1)
Tana (1)
Tanana (5)
White Seal (1)

1906

Crimmin (3)
D.R. Campbell (1)
Delta (3)
Dusty Diamond (1)
Ella (15)
Florence S. (4)
Ida May (3)
Isabelle (1)
John L. Healy (4)
Koyukuk (3)
Lavelle Young (6)
Margaret (3)
Monarch (3)
Oil City (1)
Portus B. Weare (6)
Prospector (1)
Pup (1)
Robert Kerr (1)
Schwatka (1)
Seattle #3 (2)
Tanana (10)
TC Powers (1)
White Seal (6)

1907

No documentation available for 1907

1908

Cudahy (1)
Delta (3)
D.R. Campbell (1)
Evelyn (4)
Florence S. (7)
Hamilton (3)
Jeff C. Davis (2)

John C. Barr (7)
John P. Healy (6)
J.P. Light (5)
Julia B. (1)
Koyukuk (3)
Lavelle Young (2)
Little Delta (3)
Luella (2)
Martha Clow (6)
Monarch (3)
Portus B. Weare (3)
Pup (1)
Reliance (10)
Robert Kerr (2)
Schwatka (8)
Seattle #3 (1)
Tana (4)
Tanana (18)
White Seal (12)

1909

Delta (5)
D.R. Campbell (3)
Evelyn (5)
Florence S. (1)
General J.W. Jacobs (3)
Hamilton (4)
Jeff C. Davis (1)
John L. Healy (2)
J.P. Light (1)
Julia B. (2)
Koyukuk (8)
Little Delta (2)
Luella (2)
Martha Clow (4)
Minneapolis (2)
Pup (2)
Reliance (3)
St. Michael (1)
Schwatka (9)
Seattle #3 (1)
Tana (3)
Tanana (16)
White Seal (4)

1910

Delta (1)
General J.W. Jacob (1)
John L. Healy (1)
Julia B. (1)
Koyukuk (3)
Martha Clow (3)
Minneapolis (2)
Monarch (2)
Reliance (3)
Robert Kerr (1)
Schwatka (4)
Seattle #3 (4)
Tana (2)
Tanana (6)
Teddy H. (1)
White Seal (4)

1911

Delta (1)
Evelyn (1)
General J.W. Jacob (2)
Jeff C. Davis (1)
J.P. Light (1)
Julia B. (3)
Martha Clow (4)
Minneapolis (2)
Monarch (4)
Portus B. Weare (2)
Reliance (1)
Robert Kerr (1)
Schwatka (7)
Tana (3)

Tanana (8)
Tetlin (2)
White Seal (4)

1912

Delta (2)
Evelyn (1)
General J.W. Jacob (3)
Julia B. (2)
Martha Clow (1)
Minneapolis (1)
Monarch (1)
Reliance (2)
Robert Kerr (2)
St. Michael (1)
Schwatka (2)
Tana (1)
Tanana (8)
Tetlin (2)
White Seal (3)

1913

Alaska (2)
Delta (2)
Florence S.(1)
General J.W. Jacob (1)
Julia B. (1)
Little Delta (1)
Martha Clow (1)
Minneapolis (1)
Reliance (2)
Robert Kerr (1)
Selkirk (1)
St. Michael (1)
Schwatka (1)
Tana (1)
Tanana (6)
White Seal (2)
Yukon (2)

1914

Alaska (5)
Atlas (1)
Delta (2)
Florence S.(1)
General J.W. Jacob (2)
Julia B. (3)
Martha Clow (1)
Minneapolis (2)
Reliance (1)
Robert Kerr (1)
S & S (1)
Selkirk (4)
Schwatka (3)
Shusana (4)
Tana (1)
Tanana (8)
White Seal (3)
Yukon (5)

1915

Alaska (5)
Atlas (1)
Columbus (1)
Delta (4)
General J.W. Jacob (4)
Julia B. (2)
Minneapolis (1)
Reliance (2)
Schwatka (1)
Tana (2)
Tanana (7)
Yukon (8)

1916

Alaska (5)
Atlas (1)
Dawson (1)

Delta (3)
General J.W. Jacob (2)
Julia B. (2)
Reliance (4)
Shusana (2)
Tanana (12)
Yukon (6)

1917

Alaska (7)
Alice (2)
Canadian (4)
General J.W. Jacob (3)
Julia B. (2)
Minneapolis (2)
Reliance (6)
Schwatka (1)
Seattle #3 (3)
Selkirk (1)
Shusana (2)
Tanana (6)
Teddy H. (1)
Yukon (5)

1918

Alaska (3)
General J.W. Jacob (4)
Reliance (6)
Seattle #3 (1)
Shusana (8)
Tanana (10)
Washburn (1)
Yukon (3)

1919

Alaska (6)
General J.W. Jacob (1)
Reliance (3)
Shusana (4)
Tanana (12)
Washburn (1)
Yukon (4)

1920

Alaska (3)
General J.W. Jacob (1)
Tanana (4)
Washburn (1)
Yukon (3)

1921

Alaska (2)
Carl White (1)
General J.W. Jacob (1)
Nabesna (1)
Reliance (1)
Tanana (10)
Yukon (1)

1922

No record of arrivals listed

---

* These data are derived from newspaper accounts of the day. Obviously, boats were arriving in the area prior to 1903, but we begin our count with the first newspaper issued in Fairbanks which was on September 19, 1903. From then through 1922 we used various newspapers as our source.

The number of available issues covering the steamboat season for each of these years varied from one issue in 1903 to nearly one for each day in the later years. Coincident with the waning of river traffic, the newspapers available for the period 1918-1922 carried few notices of steamboats arriving in or leaving from Fairbanks. There may have been more boats running, but it is sad commentary that river transportation had so diminished in importance. We acknowledge that we may have occasionally missed a report in a newspaper of a visit of a vessel or, indeed, we may have omitted a vessel altogether. However, to the best of our ability with the documentary sources used, we believe this to be the most extensive and accurate such list to date.

Notes

Introduction

[1] Cecil F. Robe, *The Penetration of an Alaskan Frontier, The Tanana Valley and Fairbanks* (Ph.D. dissertation, Yale University, 1943), pp. 17-20.
[2] Robe, pp. 21-22
[3] Robe, p. 23
[4] Robe, pp. 26-27
[5] Robe, pp. 68-70. Information extracted from field notebooks, journals, etc., of Alfred H. Brooks.
[6] Robe, pp. 65-67
[7] "First Voyage of Tanana Chief," *Alaska-Yukon Magazine*, II (sic), p. 557

Chapter 1

[1] Robert L. Monahan, *A Development of Settlement in the Fairbanks Area, Alaska. The Study of Permanence* (Ph.D. dissertation, McGill University, 1959), p. 51
[2] Terrence Cole, *E.T. Barnette, The Strange Story of the Man Who Founded Fairbanks* (Anchorage, Alaska: Northwest Publishing Company, 1981), pp. 18-19
[3] Cole, *E.T. Barnette,* pp. 20-21
[4] Cole, *E.T. Barnette,* pp. 20-23
[5] Cole, *E.T. Barnette,* p. 24

Chapter 2

[1] Captain C.W. Adams, as told to Robert Hazelleaf, "I Hauled 'Fairbanks' on a Sternwheeler", *Alaska Sportsman*, September 1961, p. 15

[2] Over the years, the word "Chena" has occasioned much discussion, particularly as to its spelling and meaning. Older newspapers and texts often give the spelling as "Chenoa." Early White settlers generally pronounced the word as "Shenaw." The word almost surely is derived from the Athabascan Indian term — *Ch'eno.'* The "Ch'" is an indefinite subject descriptor, possibly denoting "main." The "eno'" means "river." Therefore, it is conceivable that the word we now know as "Chena" means something approximating "main river," probably referring to the "main river for fishing, or hunting, or camping."

[3] Cole, *E.T. Barnette,* p.22

[4] Robe, pp. 103-104

[5] Cole, *E.T. Barnette*, pp. 27-28

[6] There are those who strongly doubt that this trek, especially including Isabelle Barnette, occurred in this manner, or in such a short time at such low temperature and over such terrain. However, lacking solid, documentary evidence to the contrary, and knowing that Barnette did, in fact, arrive in Seattle that spring to buy the *Isabelle*, we will stick with the version given by Terrence Cole in his book, *E.T. Barnette.* We also note that "Steamboat Bill" Heckman made the same trip in about one-half the time that it took the Barnettes. We believe the time given is feasible.

[7] Robe, pp. 122-123

[8] Cole, *E.T. Barnette,* p. 32

[9] Robe, pp. 123-124. Cole, *E.T. Barnette,* p. 34, lists the skipper as Edward Thompson.

[10] Cole, *E.T. Barnette,* p. 38

[11] Robe, pp. 144-145

[12] Robe, pp. 152-154

Chapter 3

[1] Percy Meaker, "The Tanana Valley of Alaska", *Alaska-Yukon Magazine*, IV, February 1908, p. 439

[2] Robe, pp. 160-161

[3] Robe, pp. 163-164

[4] Robe, p. 172

[5] Robe, p. 176

Chapter 4

[1] Robe, p. 150
[2] Cole, *E.T. Barnette*, p. 49-50
[3] Robe, p. 151
[4] Monahan, quoting Wickersham, p. 80
[5] Monahan, p. 81
[6] Monahan, p. 80
[7] Robe, p. 176
[8] Robe, p. 177
[9] Cole, *E.T. Barnette,* p. 62
[10] Robe, p. 169
[11] *Fairbanks Weekly News (FWN)*, September 19, 1903
[12] *FWN*, July 18, 1905
[13] Monahan, pp. 51-52
[14] Robe, p. 178
[15] Robe, p. 181
[16] Robe, pp. 182-183
[17] Monahan, p. 44
[18] Major-General A.W. Greely, *Handbook of Alaska, Its Resources and Attractions in 1924* (New York and London: Charles Scribner's Sons, 1925), p. 34
[19] Jo Ann Wold, *Fairbanks: The $200 Million Gold Rush Town* (Fairbanks: Wold Press, 1971) p. 14
[20] Monahan, p. 44
[21] Robe, p. 184
[22] *FWN*, September 19, 1903
[23] Robe, pp. 184-185
[24] Robe, p. 186

Chapter 5

[1] *FWN*, April 16, 1904
[2] *FWN*, July 30, 1904
[3] *FWN*, April 16, 1904
[4] Robe, p. 195
[5] Robe, p. 195
[6] *FWN*, July 30, 1904
[7] Arthur E. Knutson, *Sternwheels on the Yukon* (Kirkland, Washington: Knutson Enterprises, Inc., 1979), pp. 121-122

[8] *Fairbanks Evening News (FEN)*, August 3, 1905
[9] *FEN*, August 4, 1905
[10] *FEN*, August 9, 1905
[11] *FEN*, July 18, 1905
[12] There has been some confusion in the past about this boat, as there was apparently another *Delta* built or remodeled in 1906. Moreover there was the *Little Delta*, as well, which only confuses the matter more.

Chapter 6

[1] Robe, p. 188
[2] Cole, *E.T. Barnette,* p. 76
[3] Robe, p. 187
[4] Robe, p. 189
[5] Monahan, p. 78. Taken from the U.S. Department of the Interior, *Mineral Industry of Alaska*, U.S. Geological Survey, various bulletins 1902-1944.
[6] *Fairbanks Daily News-Miner (FDNM)*, April 21, 1985. Extracted from 1904 City Council minutes. Monahan, p. 47, reports that a bridge to Garden Island was built in 1904 and replaced the cable ferry. Cole, *E.T. Barnette,* pp. 95-96, says the new Cushman Street Bridge was built in 1905 for $10,000 and there was also a recently built bridge at Wendell Street.
[7] Monahan, p. 47
[8] *Fairbanks Daily Times (FDT)*, April 25, 1916
[9] Robe, pp. 178-179
[10] Robe, p. 199
[11] Robe, pp. 196-198
[12] John Scudder McLain, *Alaska and the Klondike* (New York: McClure, Phillips and Co., 1905), pp. 306-307
[13] Robe, p. 198
[14] Monahan, pp. 83-84
[15] Monahan, p. 14
[16] Robe, p. 202
[17] Robe, p. 203
[18] Wold, p. 37
[19] Robe p. 203
[20] Monahan, p. 82

[21] Cole, *E.T. Barnette,* p. 84-85

Chapter 7

[1] Cole, *E.T. Barnette,* p. 82
[2] Cole, cited from the *Dawson Daily News,* September 15, 1904.
[3] Terrence Cole, *Ghosts of the Gold Rush, A Walking Tour of Fairbanks* (Fairbanks: Tanana-Yukon Historical Society, 1977), p. 6
[4] Monahan, p. 50
[5] Wold, p. 17
[6] Cole, *E.T. Barnette*, p. 84
[7] Monahan, p. 45
[8] Cole, *E.T. Barnette,* p. 87
[9] Cole, *E.T. Barnette,* p. 87
[10] Duane Koenig, "Ghost Railway in Alaska: The Story of the Tanana Valley Railroad", *Pacific Northwest Quarterly*, January 1954, pp. 8-12

Chapter 8

[1] Robe, p. 33
[2] Robe, p. 91
[3] Gordon Newell, ed., *The H.W. McCurdy Marine History of the Pacific Northwest* (Seattle: Superior Publishing Company, 1966), p. 112
[4] *FDNM*, May 12, 1920 and April 18, 1923
[5] *Alaskan Engineering Commission*, Reports of the Alaskan Engineering Commission . . . March 12, 1914 to December 31, 1915 (Washington, D.C., 1916), p. 66
[6] Sidney Paige, "A Growing Camp in the Tanana Gold Fields, Alaska", *National Geographic Magazine*, March 1905, p. 107

Chapter 9

[1] Monahan, pp. 84-85
[2] Monahan, p. 3
[3] *FDT*, August 16, 1908 and *Fairbanks Daily News (FDN)*, September 15, 1908

[4] *FDT*, May 23, 1906
[5] Knutson, p. 122
[6] *FDT*, May 23, 1906
[7] Robe, p. 12
[8] *Directory of the Tanana Valley* (Fairbanks: Tanana Directory Company, 1907), p. 116-117
[9] *FEN* , September 6, 1906
[10] *Directory,* p. 25
[11] *Fairbanks Daily News (FDN)*, June 7, 1908
[12] *FDN,* June 14, 1908
[13] *FDN,* June 26, 1908
[14] *FDN,* September 10, 1908
[15] *FDN,* July 24, 1908
[16] *Directory*, p. 23
[17] Monahan, pp. 52-53
[18] *FDNM,* August 12, 1909
[19] *Alaskan Engineering Commission,* p. 66
[20] Paige, p. 108
[21] *FDN*, September 8, 1908
[22] Joe King, "The Tanana Valley", *Alaska-Yukon Magazine*, VIII, No. 4, January 1909, p. 255
[23] *FEN*, September 10, 1906
[24] *FDT*, May 14 – May 27, 1909
[25] *FDT*, May 25, 1909
[26] *FDT*, May 25, 1909
[27] *FDT*, May 18, 1909
[28] *FDNM,* April 5, 1909
[29] *FEN*, August 8, 1906
[30] *FDN*, July 25, 1908
[31] *FDN*, October 18, 1908

Chapter 10

[1] *FDNM*, September 17, 1909
[2] *FDN*, June 7, 1908
[3] *FDNM*, September 17, 1909
[4] *FDT*, June 12, 1909
[5] *FDNM*, September 4, 1909
[6] *FDNM*, September 4, 1909
[7] *FEN*, October 16, 1906

[8] *FDN*, July 25, 1908
[9] *FDT*, June 4, 1909
[10] *FDT*, June, 1909

Chapter 11

[1] *FEN* September 14, 1906
[2] The Navigability Studies paper "Lower Tanana River," Storet Number 16033997005001230 0 Typescript. Bureau of Land Management (Anchorage, p. 3) n.d. said in 1907 the N.N.C. and N.T. & T. annually carried about 25,000 tons with considerably more carried by the independent steamers. The *Fairbanks Daily Times*, August 9, 1908, says 32,000 tons per year.
[3] Monahan, pp. 44-45
[4] Janet Matheson and F. Bruce Haldeman, *Historic Resources in the Fairbanks North Star Borough* (Fairbanks: Fairbanks North Star Borough, 1981), p. 31
[5] *FDN*, September 18, 1908
[6] *FDT*, May 27, 1909
[7] *FEN*, August 28, 1906
[8] *FEN*, August 31, 1906
[9] *FEN*, August 31, 1906
[10] *FEN*, September 19, 1906
[11] *FEN*, September 27, 1906
[12] *FEN*, September 5 & 27, 1906
[13] *FDN*, June 6, 1908
[14] *FDT*, July 13, 1911
[15] *FDT*, July 7, 1908(9)
[16] *FDN*, September 13, 1908
[17] *FDN*, September 15, 1908
[18] *FDN*, September 17, 1908
[19] *FDN*, September 4 and 22, 1908
[20] *FDT*, July 11, 1909
[21] *FDNM*, October 1, 1909
[22] *FDT*, August 4, 1908
[23] *FDN*, June 22, 1908
[24] *FDN*, September 25, 1908
[25] *FDN*, October 13, 1908
[26] *FDT*, May 11 and May 26, 1909

[27] *FDT*, May 19 – June 1, 1909
[28] *FDT*, May 13 – June 1, 1909
[29] *FDT*, May 27 and June 3, 1909
[30] *FDT*, May 19 – May 27, 1909
[31] *FDT*, July 3, 1909
[32] *FDNM*, September 15 – October 9, 1909
[33] Captain Edward Heckman, "I was a Yukon Steamboat Man", *Alaska Sportsman*, December-January, 1960-61

Chapter 12

[1] Monahan, p. 100. Taken from the U.S. Department of Commerce, *U.S. Census Bureau Reports 1910-1950*, (Washington: Government Printing Office). The *Descriptive of Fairbanks* published by the Fairbanks Commercial Club in 1916 said the population was around 3,500.
[2] Robe, p. 12
[3] *Descriptive of Fairbanks "Alaska's Golden Heart"* (Fairbanks: Fairbanks Commercial Club, 1916), pp. 14-20
[4] *FDNM*, April 19, 1917
[5] Agnes Rush Burr, *Alaska, Our Beautiful Northland of Opportunity* (Boston: Page Co., 1919), p. 146
[6] *FDNM*, September 23, 1921
[7] *FDT*, August 13, 1911
[8] *FDT*, October 4, 1911
[9] *FDT*, June 5, 1915
[10] *FDT*, September 16, 1914
[11] *FDNM*, May 14 – June 2, 1917
[12] *FDT*, July 6, 1915
[13] *FDNM*, October 1, 1910
[14] *FDT*, August 26, 1911
[15] *FDT*, July 14, 1914
[16] *FDT*, July 23, 1914
[17] *Alaskan Engineering Commission Report*, p. 64
[18] *Descriptive*, p. 21
[19] *FDT*, May 3, 1911
[20] *FDT*, September 1, 1916
[21] *Descriptive*, p. 12
[22] Monahan, p. 56
[23] Hudson Stuck, *Voyages on the Yukon and its Tributaries*

(New York: Charles Scribner's Sons, 1917), p. 292
[24] *FDT*, May 7, 1913
[25] *FDT*, September 13, 1911
[26] Stuck, p. 307
[27] *FDNM*, October 3, 1916
[28] Monahan, pp. 112-124
[29] *FDT*, May 14, 1916
[30] *FDNM*, July 18, 1921
[31] *FDNM*, September, 1918

Chapter 13

[1] *Alaskan Engineering Commission*, pp. 64-65
[2] *FDT*, May 26, June 24, and July 11, 1915
[3] Monahan, p. 55
[4] Monahan, p. 56
[5] *FDNM*, May 7 – June 9, 1923
[6] Barry C. Anderson, *Lifeline to the Yukon: A History of Yukon Navigation* (Seattle: Superior Publishing, 1983), p. 69
[7] Monahan, p. 57. Extracted from Norman L. Wimmler's *Placer Mining Methods and Costs*, 1927.
[8] Anderson, p. 69

Chapter 14

[1] *FDNM*, April 29, 1910
[2] *FDNM*, June 2, 1910
[3] *FDT*, May 19, 1911
[4] Stan Cohen, *Yukon River Steamboats, A Pictorial History* (Missoula, Montana: Pictorial Histories Publishing Company, 1982), p. 112
[5] *FDT*, June 11, 1913
[6] *FDT*, May 28 and Jul.y 18, 1915
[7] *FDT*, June 22, 1913
[8] Knutson, p. 15
[9] Melody Webb, "Steamboats on the Yukon River", *Alaska Journal,* XV, Summer 1985, p. 28
[10] Anderson, p. 66
[11] *FDT*, April 30, 1914
[12] *FDT*, July 15, 1914

[13] *FDT*, May 22, 1914
[14] *FDT*, October 8, 1914
[15] *FDT*, June 3, 1915
[16] *FDT*, April 25, 1916
[17] *FDT*, September 1, 1914
[18] Anderson, p. 69
[19] *FDT*, June 30, 1912
[20] *FDT*, May 7, 1913
[21] *FDNM*, May 14, 1917

Some Concluding Thoughts

[1] T. Cole, *Ghosts*, p. 30
[2] Memorandum of Decision, Civil Action No. 62-388

References

1961 Adams, Captain C.W. as told to Robert Hazelleaf. "I Hauled 'Fairbanks' on a Sternwheeler." *Alaska Sportsman*, September, pp. 14-15.

1916 *Alaskan Engineering Commission.* Reports of the Alaskan Engineering Commission.... March 12, 1914 to December 31, 1915. Washington, D.C.

1983 Anderson, Barry C. *Lifeline to the Yukon: A History of Yukon Navigation.* Seattle: Superior Publishing.

1919 Burr, Agnes Rush. *Alaska Our Beautiful Northland of Opportunity.* Boston: Page Company.

1982 Cohen, Stan. *Yukon River Steamboats, A Pictorial History.* Missoula, Montana: Pictorial Histories Publishing Company.

1981 Cole, Terrence. *E.T. Barnette, The Strange Story of the Man Who Founded Fairbanks.* Anchorage, Alaska: Alaska Northwest Publishing Company.

1977 Cole, Terrence. *Ghosts of the Gold Rush, A Walking Tour of Fairbanks.* Fairbanks, Alaska: Tanana-Yukon Historical Society.

1954 Cooley, Richard A. *Fairbanks Alaska, A Survey of Progress.* Juneau, Alaska: Alaska Development Board.

1916 *Descriptive of Fairbanks "Alaska's Golden Heart."* Fairbanks, Alaska: Fairbanks Commercial Club.

1907 *Directory of the Tanana Valley.* Fairbanks, Alaska: Tanana Directory Company.

1908 *Fairbanks Daily News.* June, July, September, October 1908.

Various *Fairbanks Daily News Miner.* April 3-5, August, September, October 1909; June, August and October, 1910; May 12, 1920; April-October 1921; May-July 1923; April 21, 1985.

Various *Fairbanks Daily Times.* May 23, 1906, August 1908; April-July 1909; May, July-October 1911; May, June, August 1912; May, June, August-October 1913; March-July, September, October 1914; April 27-September 1915; April-October 1916.

1906 *Fairbanks Evening News.* July, August, 1905; August-October 1906.

1908 *Fairbanks Sunday Times.* August 2, 1908

Various *Fairbanks Weekly News.* September 19, 1903; April 16 and July 30, 1904; July, August, September 1905.

1925 Greely, Major-General A.W. *Handbook of Alaska, Its Resources and Attractions in 1924.* New York and London: Charles Scribner's Sons.

1960-61 Heckman, Captain Edward. "I Was a Yukon Steamboat Man." *Alaska Sportsman.* December, 1960 and January 1961.

1909 King, Joe. "The Tanana Valley." *Alaska-Yukon Magazine.* Vol VIII, No. 4, January, pp. 251-258.

1979 Knutson, Arthur E. *Sternwheels on the Yukon.* Kirkland, Washington: Knutson Enterprises, Inc.

1954 Koenig, Duane. "Ghost Railway in Alaska: The Story of the Tanana Valley Railroad." *Pacific Northwest Quarterly.* January, pp. 8-12

1981 Matheson, Janet and F. Bruce Haldeman. *Historic Resources in the Fairbanks North Star Borough.* Fairbanks, Alaska: Fairbanks North Star Borough.

1905 McLain, John Scudder. *Alaska and the Klondike.* New York: McClure, Phillips and Company.

1908 Meaker, Percy. "The Tanana Valley of Alaska." *Alaska-Yukon Magazine*, Vol. IV, February, pp. 437-448.

1959 Monahan, Robert Leonard. *The Development of Settlement in the Fairbanks Area, Alaska. A Study of Permanence.* Ph.D. dissertation, McGill University.

1965 *Memorandum of Decision.* State of Alaska, Plaintiff vs. Walt Wigger and Morton deLima Company, Inc., Defendants. Civil Action No. 62-388. January 29, 1965. Fairbanks, Alaska.

1909 n.a., "First Voyage of the Tanana Chief." *Alaska-Yukon Magazine.* Vol. II [sic], March, pp. 555-557.

1966 Newell, Gordon, ed., *The H.W. McCurdy Marine History of the Pacific Northwest.* Seattle: Superior Publishing Company.

1905 Paige, Sidney. "A Growing Camp in the Tanana Gold Fields, Alaska." *National Geographic Magazine.* March, pp. 104-111.

1909 Richard, T.A. *Through the Yukon and Alaska.* San Francisco: Mining and Scientific Press.

1943 Robe, Cecil Francis. *The Penetration of an Alaskan Frontier, The Tanana Valley and Fairbanks.* Ph.D. dissertation, Yale University.

1917 Stuck, Hudson. *Voyages on the Yukon and its Tributaries.* New York: Charles Scribner's Sons.

1902 *34th Annual List of Merchant Vessels of the United States.* Washington: Government Printing Office.

1903 *35th Annual List of Merchant Vessels of the United States.* Washington: Government Printing Office.

U.S. Department of Interior. Bureau of Land Management. *Lower Tanana River.* Navigability studies paper Storet Number 16033997005001230 0 Typescript. Anchorage (no date).

1985 Webb, Melody. "Steamboats on the Yukon River." *Alaska Journal.* Vol. XV, Summer, pp. 21-29.

1971 Wold, Jo Ann. *Fairbanks: the $200 Million Gold Rush Town.* Fairbanks, Alaska: Wold Press.

Dr. Basil "Base" Hedrick is the only direct descendant of a life-long Mississippi River captain. Hedrick, who has traveled and worked around the world in many academic and administrative capacities, once worked as a deckhand and fireman on a sternwheeler steamboat. Hedrick served as director of the University of Alaska Museum in Fairbanks from 1980 to 1988, when he was named director of the Michigan State Museum system.

Born on Saint Patrick's Day in 1932, Base has lived abroad and earned his doctoral degree in Mexico where he lived for several years. He has been a teacher, museum director, dean of international education as well as cook, truck driver and student. He is married to Susan Pickel-Hedrick.

Susan Savage was born in 1943 and was raised in a small rural community near Detroit, Michigan, graduating from Albion College in 1964 with a degree in math and biology. She married her husband, Jerry Savage, and moved to Alaska that same year.

Since 1973, the couple has lived in a log cabin they built about 30 miles east of Fairbanks where they keep one horse, one goat, two dogs, two cats and two parakeets.

Soon after the Savages moved to Fairbanks, they bought an Athabascan rat canoe, used to hunt muskrat, and used it to travel extensively along the Chena, Tanana, Yukon and Chatanika rivers. After the birth of their two girls, Sarah and Jennifer, they replaced the Indian canoe with a clumsy but roomier aluminum canoe.